More praise for '1972'

Steve Bence, a nationally ranked 800 meter runner and 40-plus year teammate of mine at Nike, brings a unique perspective on the Nike story. I enjoyed his book, and think you will, too.

—Phil Knight
Nike cofounder

Who would have thought it would be possible to plow fresh ground amidst the larger stories of Pre, Bowerman, Knight and Nike? But along comes Steve Bence, a former 800-meter runner who walked on at Oregon in the fall of 1971. He competed for Bowerman, considered Pre one of his closest friends, and when his unlikely UO career came to a close, he signed on to help Nike establish its early overseas operations. Now, a half-century later, Bence provides an insider's view of those iconic figures and company with an authentic voice that takes readers on an emotional ride filled with rollicking tales and somber reflection. A wonderful read that left me wanting more.

—Curtis Anderson
TrackTown USA/OTC Elite Press Officer
and former sports reporter at *The Register-Guard*

The classic hope of any writer is to find the most perfect words for telling a story; the French have it right, "le mot juste." Yet, over and over, Steve Bence does that, even more than that in telling his take on history as a runner at University of Oregon and as an early employee at Nike. Every time he asserts he is not a writer, his text proves otherwise. Every time he avers he is not the right historian to define Bill Bowerman, Phil Knight or Steve Prefontaine, his knowing stories prove the opposite.

—Kenny Moore
Olympic marathoner, former *Sports Illustrated* writer

D1596996

Bence's story is full of heart, offering stories that create a movie in one's mind about why Nike is Nike and why the people who live and work at Nike carry a special feeling about what they're doing. This book is a gift. Anyone who reads 1972 will see that anything is possible if you follow your heart and believe in what the spirit of an athlete and the heart of a coach can do together—or one skinny kid in oversized running shoes can do in a lifetime.

—Patrice Thramer
Former University of Oregon
basketball player and longtime Nike leader

A fascinating, authentic look into the people and culture that contributed to the growth of Nike and of Track Town USA. A must-read!

—Tom Jordan
Author of *PRE*
The Story of America's Greatest Running Legend

A personal story, a sports story, a business story, a passion story, beautifully told, by a man who lived every word of it.

—Jeff Johnson
Nike's first full-time employee

Life tells the best stories and this touching book invites you to join Steve Bence, this humble and motivating "Runner for a lifetime," on his vivid memories of icons like Pre and on Bence's early days at Nike. Get inspired by him embracing lifelong flexibility, adaptability, and dealing with change—and simply enjoy this run!

—Jessica Meyer
Nikeplay leader, Nike Singapore

Steve Bence is tenacious. He is also loyal, smart, funny, kind, and honest. In his autobiography, all these characteristics are apparent. They radiate out of every sentence. Nothing is hidden in the seams. He tells his whole story, his truth. Anyone who is interested in those stories of how Nike came to be and how a half-miler could evolve into a marathoner with time and tenacity will love this book. I did.

Mary Marckx Creel
Retired raconteur, friend of Pre and Bence

I loved the book! It's a running-geek story, a wonderful, easy-to-read life story written by a talented and dedicated man. It's a personal story that will make you smile, cry, and cheer.

—Nelson Farris
Third-most tenured Nike employee
and unofficial "keeper of the Nike culture"

Steve Bence

Jeff Johnson

STEVE BENCE   STEVE PREFONTAINE

OREGON - UCLA - NEBRASKA - WASHINGTON STATE

HAYWARD FIELD   SATURDAY, APRIL 14, 1973   25c

Top: In September 1972, on my first day in Eugene, I walked into Coach Bill Dellinger's office and was stunned to see two stars: Jim Ryun, in town training for the Olympics in Munich, and Steve Prefontaine. Like a gawking fan, I asked if I could take a quick photo. Ryun had a little of the "Clark Kent" look going. I was clueless about the dude in the striped pants, some guy named Phil. Above: Me as a sopho-more, 1973. Right: Making a program cover with Pre that same year.

1972

Pre, UO Track, Nikes Shoes, and My Life with Them All

Steve Bence

with Bob Welch

SB4 Press
Beaverton, Oregon

SB4 Press, Beaverton, Oregon

Second edition
050322 printing

Front cover: On April 1, 1972, exactly one month before Nike officially launched, University of Oregon freshman walk-on Steve Bence won the 800 meters—Olympic-year distance—in his first race at Hayward Field in Eugene. The event was the Oregon Invitational, his time 1:49.2. (Photo used with permission of UO Libraries Special Collections & University Archives. Index: "Steve Bence, A_ATHTF_Mens1970s_0017, University Archives photographs, UA Ref 3, UO Libraries Special Collections & University Archives.")

Front and back cover designs by Bob Welch and Tom Penix, PenWax Designs.

ISBN: 978-0-9772306-3-1

To contact the author: SteveBence@icloud.com

Printed in the United States of America

To my teammates and competitors
and to all who carry the spirit of sport.
We push each other to become the best that we can be.

And to those who've shared my Nike journey—
co-workers, business partners, and friends.
Our work is more than just a job.
For us, there is no finish line.

Contents

Author's Note

In 2020, when co-founder Phil Knight set the official date for Nike's fiftieth anniversary in two years, I was reminded of what an incredible history this iconic company has had. And how privileged I was to have been even a small slice of the Nike pizza.

When that thought nudged me to consider telling my version of the Nike story in a book, however, I immediately recoiled, as if a runner who had false started. Wasn't I getting ahead of myself? What right did I have to think I deserved such a platform? I'm no writer. And I've never been a top executive or even a fascinating footnote like Carolyn Davidson, the Portland State graphic design student who designed the swoosh in 1971—for $35. Hey, I'm just a numbers nerd who caught a great wave and am still smiling as I ride it to shore.

But then a friend pointed out that of the nearly 500,000 people who have worked for the company since its official inception on May 1, 1972, I have outlasted all but four. That I ran for the legendary Bill Bowerman at the University of Oregon, considered Steve Prefontaine among my closest friends, and was among the first handful of employees to set up manufacturing operations overseas. That in the last twenty-five years, I'd led more than a hundred heritage tours for employees to the UO, Hayward Field, and Pre's Rock. And, finally, that I recently began teaching second-year MBA and UO Sports Product Management graduate students about the industry.

In 2019, I was chosen by Senior Vice President Mike Brewer to lead the effort to tell Nike's manufacturing story in a video. Said Greg Bui, vice president of Global Sourcing and Manufacturing (GSM): "After 42 years of 'having his fingerprints all over this company' (a quote from our founder Phil Knight), we think Steve is uniquely qualified. Steve's love for Nike is infectious and so is his passion for GSM."

After assembling a support team of 10 people, I led the work for about 18 months. By the end of the project, we had interviewed 67 people on camera in the US, Korea, Taiwan, and Japan, producing a 45-minute documentary.

I started the story in 1964—the year of the Tokyo Olympics—when Phil Knight placed his first order for 300 pair of shoes to Japan, and book-ended the story with the 2021 return of the Covid-delayed Olympics to Tokyo. In between, we told of the manufacturing partnership we built and maintained between Nike and Asia over those 57 years.

Context, it's been said, is everything. To understand the company's start in 1964 requires understanding Knight, Bowerman, and Bill Hayward, plus the legacy of track and field in Oregon, the great athletes, and Bowerman's tinkering that led to breakthrough innovations. Much of which I was not only an eyewitness to, but part of.

So, this story is my personal addendum to that larger one. Part Nike. Part me. A tapestry of the two, really. I want to tell it not for any egocentric reason but for the sake of historic preservation. To not tell your story, it's been said, is to let that story die—and to rob the next generation of something they might learn from. So, to that end, this is my small contribution.

It's not a comprehensive history of Nike. It's not me speaking for anyone else. It's simply my prelude to life at Nike—my running career at Oregon—and the manufacturing side of Nike, particularly in the early days, that I know. Nothing more. Nothing less. Me. Forty-four years. And a company that, according to Phil, was born on a spring day in 1972 when I couldn't have been feeling much better about myself as an athlete or as a human being.

Not that, at the time, I'd even heard of Nike. Or, for that matter, Phil Knight.

—Steve Bence
Beaverton, Oregon
September 2021

Prologue

When I awakened in my University of Oregon dorm room on Monday, May 1, 1972—the day Nike was technically launched—life was sweet. Oh, the country was going to hell in a handbasket. The war in Vietnam raged. The protests back home roiled. And those of us in the dorm were worrying about our draft numbers. But I was riding high.

For years unrest had rocked the UO campus, among its victims, interim school president Chuck Johnson, who had had an emotional breakdown because of the volatility. In 1969, he was killed on the McKenzie Highway when he swerved his VW into an oncoming logging truck; whether he was trying to take his life or not, his death epitomized the signs of strained times.

But, personally, I was transcending the turmoil. Though I had little sense that it would last, an uneasy peace had descended on campus. I, too, was at peace. A half-miler, I'd won my first six races at the country's premiere distance-running school—as a freshman walk-on who, truth be told, no school had wanted, not even Oregon. But I was starting to earn respect, not only from my legendary distance-running coach, Bill Bowerman, but from my teammates and fans, nearly 10,000 of whom would pack Hayward Field to watch our team compete on Saturdays.

Unbelievable. I was an Air Force brat who'd been living in Spain, where my father had been stationed, and where I would win races on dirt tracks in front of a dozen onlookers, half of whom didn't know track from field. Now, I was in heaven, hitting my stride—literally—as an eighteen-year-old unknown running alongside the nation's most celebrated distance runner, Steve Prefontaine. A photo of him running near Bowerman's house in the Coburg Hills had recently graced the cover of *Sports Illustrated.*

"Hell, Bence, you keep this up and you might actually earn a scholarship," Pre told me in Nebraska after I'd narrowly won my fifth race.

I was in the proverbial groove. And looking forward to the coming Saturday's home dual meet against Oregon's archrival, Oregon State, whose coach, Berny Wagner, had politely rebuffed me when I'd accidentally sent an introductory letter to OSU, thinking it was Oregon.

"You'd need get your time down to 1:52 to have any hope of even a partial scholarship," he'd written.

Now, I was slated to face off with OSU's standout Hailu Ebba, an Ethiopian who was as experienced as I was not. He'd run 1:48.9; I'd done 1:49.4. *The (Eugene) Register-Guard* headline said it all: "Bence vs. Ebba in Civil War."

Since I'd stepped on campus in the fall, the experience had all seemed like a dream.

One Friday night, while everyone else in the dorm was

partying, I walked over to Hayward Field and, high in the stands, sat alone, soaking in the view. The air was cool and clean, unlike late summer in the southern Willamette Valley when farmers burned off their fields and smoke hung like smoky fog for days. I could hear the sound of a school band in the distance—from a football game at nearby South Eugene High. And, from the dorms just north of the track and field complex, I could hear a mish-mash of blaring music—from Carole King's "It's Too Late" to Jackson Browne's "Doctor My Eyes" to Neil Young's "Heart of Gold."

Was I really here, running for Bowerman, the guy who'd led Oregon to four NCAA track and field championships and produced eleven sub-four-minute milers? Who madly cobbled shoes at night in hopes that he might create a style that would be lighter and faster than what we were using? Who was considered America's "Father of Jogging?"

On that fall evening, in the Hayward Field stands, I vowed to do my best. It was as if I'd felt so lucky to even be here in the first place that I dared not waste the opportunity.

The music from the dorms pounded, the band played on at South Eugene. But soon I'd blotted both from my mind. Instead, I was thinking back to Spain and to a childhood that never promised the kind of dream I was now living at the University of Oregon.

On grounds in Nuremberg, Germany where Hitler parades were once held, I won the 800 meters in the 1971 United States Dependents Schools, European Areas (USDESEA) Championships in meet-record time of 1:55.2—after a coach from another team loaned me a pair of size 9 Adidas spikes. Following the semifinal heat, the coach was stunned that I had run so well in a clunky pair of U.S.-made Wilson spikes, right, that were two sizes too large. My mother had approved the latter, thinking they would allow me room to "grow into."

PART I

RUNNING

You have brains in your head.
You have feet in your shoes.
You can steer yourself any
direction you choose.

—Dr. Seuss

Chapter 1
An Unknown in Oversized Shoes

I was born in Tennessee, started kindergarten in Japan, and graduated high school in Spain. I lived in ten cities and three countries over those years, and I was in different high schools my sophomore, junior, and senior years.

Ah, the life of an Air Force kid.

School wasn't that hard; what was hard was remembering my latest address. Making friends with people while knowing that I wasn't going to be around long enough to keep those friendships. Planning anything beyond a few months out seemed impossible.

Why? Because I never knew when Dad was going to give us our latest "orders." And they almost always involved leaving where we were and going somewhere else where the Air Force wanted him to be.

No wonder I grew up as a kid desperately trying to find a

place to belong. To feel some sort of permanence. To feel as if I mattered.

In school, of course, among the arenas in which you could find that sense of belonging was sports—especially if you were a boy. (Girls were given few athletic opportunities in the days before Title IX, in 1972, which required equal opportunities be offered to females in federally funded institutes). But early on, there was no indiciation that sports were going to be the answer to my question of belonging.

In sixth grade, we ran a one-mile course in a physical education class, an endeavor that I enjoyed. Running felt easy. Being out in front was fun. But such feel-good moments were the exception to the "you-stink" moments involving other sports I tried.

In seventh grade, when we lived on Edwards Air Force Base, California, I played football and basketball because my friends did. I mainly rode the bench. Once, in the waning minutes, I was sent into a basketball game whose outcome had already been decided. Four straight times I brought the ball up the court; four straight times I committed a dribbling violation. I glanced at the bench; my coach was shaking his head.

Just my luck; he was also my track and field coach in the spring. He did his best to ignore me. I worked hard. I wanted to race. But each week when he posted the names of those who were going to be competing in each of the events, mine wasn't there. If basketball had taught me that I was a loser, track and field wasn't doing anything to prove otherwise. Every week, I'd scan the list. Every week, I'd feel the rejection.

Then, just before the district championships, Coach came up to me.

"Bence," he said. "You're running the 440."

What? Was this some sort of joke? Was I being set up? Or was this just a token "bone" he'd thrown to me because we had a weak quarter-mile lineup? Perhaps it was a way to alleviate his guilt, getting me into one race, since I worked as hard as anyone else.

But, surprisingly, I finished second in district! Then, as if I'd been invisible all season and he'd suddenly seen me for the first time, he rushed over and embraced me while I was trying to recover from the race.

"Bence," he said, "you're a runner!"

I was almost as surprised as he was. But the label stuck. I became known as just that, "a runner," competing in cross-county and track. As a sophomore, I won the 660 in the district championships, advancing to the first round of the California Southern Section championships. In any sport, that was a pretty big accomplishment for our Desert High School on Edwards Air Force Base—yeah, the place where the Space Shuttle would one day be tested and land after its missions. I advanced through the preliminary rounds, breaking the school record, and made it to the finals, where I finished third. At our final school assembly of 300 students, I was recognized for my accomplishment, and received a standing ovation. It was surreal.

And then—to no real surprise—our family moved. Again.

This time it was to Torrejon Air Force Base in Spain, where I didn't know anyone and nobody knew me. My sudden sense of significance vanished overnight, just one more remnant of life as an Air Force brat. But I started to claw my way back; running became my passport to acceptance.

In early summer, we moved into Royal Oaks, the base housing. I took a lifeguard job on the main base, where the younger airmen who lived in the barracks used the pool to blow off some steam. Friday nights were often party nights, and the cleanup involved my diving into the pool to fish out the floating beer cans, the number of which was considerable. The job kept me from meeting people my own age over the summer, but it did provide spending money.

Madrid American High School didn't have a cross country team because there wasn't enough interest to field a seven-

runner team, so, as a junior, I decided to play football, mainly
for conditioning. I let the coaches know I was a runner, which
translated to "running back." But I rarely got in a game. The
star running back—the guy who got the playing time that
eluded me—was also the star on the track team, a middle-
distance runner, so I turned a few heads when we ran a mile on
the track, in helmets, and I beat him and everyone else.

The head football coach, Bill Elstran, was also my math
teacher.

"Bence, that was a pretty impressive mile yesterday," he said.
"That's where your talent is." So, apparently, I'd once again been
"discovered."

He knew me, it felt good. He encouraged me to skip
winter sports and ask the P.E. and track coach, Mr. Wynn, for
workouts, which I did. When track and field season arrived,
I found myself running on a track that was nothing more
than squiggly chalk lines on packed dirt. Our district was
composed of our school, Madrid American High school—the
largest—and the schools at Morón AFB and Rota Naval Base
in southern Spain, plus Kenitra Naval Base in Morocco. The
highlight of the season was an impromptu meet with a Spanish
track club on our home track and then our district meet, at
which I won the 800 meters by 15 seconds. That qualified me
to run at the All-Europe Championship Meet in Germany,
officially the United States Dependents Schools, European
Areas (USDESEA) Championships.

From the time I stepped off the plane, I found Germany
spectacular. Trees, fresh air, more modern than Spain, and
so well-organized. I knew the Germans had a reputation for
engineering and structure, and I could see it on the streets,
including the efficiently running traffic.

The meet was held on a beautiful track in Nuremberg, in
a place that had apparently been a favorite rally grounds for
Adolf Hitler and his speeches. In fact, in 1938, with swastikas
flying everywhere, 80,000 youth—boys and girls the same ages

I was—had gathered here to pay homage to the man in a week-long rally culminated with their marching in formation to spell out A-D-O-L-F—H-I-T-L-E-R.

Now, the area had been converted into a medium-sized park, including the track. The meet drew athletes from all the military base schools in Europe; the biggest schools were in Germany and England. In the prelims alone, I realized how good the competition was. I had to run a school-record 1:59.2 just to advance to the finals, the lone member of our team to get past the semis.

A coach from one of the larger schools in Germany—he'd never even heard of me—told my coach how impressed he'd been with my effort. Then he saw my spikes.

"You ran under two minutes in those?"

They were a pair of Wilson red leather spikes that my mother had bought for me in California three years before, when I was a freshman. The salesman had measured my feet and said I should buy size 11. The shoes felt big at the time, but my mother was happy that there was plenty of room for my feet to grow and encouraged me to get them. Not, of course, that she was having to run in them.

"They're far too big for him," the coach said.

Indeed, I was about to run the European finals in a boardy, heavy, over-sized pair of spikes. (In college, I would wear size 9 or smaller.)

"Give me a minute," the coach said.

He soon returned with a beautiful pair of blue and white Adidas spikes.

"Try these."

It was my introduction to shoes, something my life would soon revolve around. I had no idea what a difference a pair of shoes could make. They were light and snug; I felt faster just putting them on.

I won the 800 in 1:56.3, three seconds faster than my previous best the day before and a new record for European high schools for US military kids.

Back at school, Coach Elstran was thrilled.

"Class, I have to tell you what an incredible accomplishment Bence achieved while representing our school," he said. He went on and on about me, which did wonders for my confidence, especially coming from him. The highly respected football coach was validating my track accomplishment in front of my classmates.

And then, of course, my father was transferred—a line that accompanies almost any early Steve Bence story.

We moved to Morón AFB near Seville in southern Spain. The base was put on caretaker status, one step away from shutting down completely. At the same time, Zaragoza AFB in northern Spain was reactivated as a training and practice run for fighter pilots in the European region. Along with my sophomore brother Randy, I didn't know where we'd be attending school. The rumors were that Morón HS was shutting down and a decision would be announced in August about how they would handle our schooling. My mother feared her two sons would be leaving home to attend some sort of boarding school before she was ready to have us leave the house.

The final decision to operate a high school in Zaragoza was made on August 12, 1970. Randy and I would be going there. Three days later truckloads of supplies began to roll in and the school was taking shape. Teachers and administrators were assigned. Contractors repaired the dormant high school. Two barracks were turned into boys' and girls' dormitories. The military knew how to move material, equipment, and personnel, including us kids. Less than three weeks after the announcement, Randy and I, now labeled as among the "dormies" by the locals, moved in on separate floors, making intentional efforts to stay connected and supportive.

Later that fall, the Stars and Stripes newspaper wrote, "Zaragoza is USDESEA's newest high school but it already has a sports hero in Steve Bence. The school didn't field a football team but it had quite a runner in Bence and coach Ron Uhl said they just had to have a cross country team with a runner like Steve in school. He traveled to Germany for the USDESEA cross country finals and finished second to Wuerzburg's Charlie Hill."

A major priority my senior year was finding a college. I was accepted academically to the colleges I applied to: Ohio State, Kent State, Kansas State, USC, and Oregon State. But the letters from the track coaches were not encouraging.

Vern Wolfe, USC's head coach, wrote bluntly, "Your time is a dime a dozen in southern California. We have to be selective, or we could never survive in the Pac-8 and at the national level."

Discouraged, I turned to one of the dorm counselors, Jim Sagle, for help; he had thrown the javelin at the University of Oregon.

"I'm probably going to go to Kansas State," I told him.

"Why there?"

"Because I want to go to the same college as Jim Ryun."

"Ryun went to Kansas, not Kansas State."

"Oh! I thought the universities with 'State' in them were the main colleges."

Wrong assumption; Kansas State was out.

"Oregon State?" he asked. "Why is that on your list?"

"Isn't that where you went to school? It sounded like a great university for runners."

"No, I went to the University of Oregon. That's where you want to go. Bill Bowerman has a walk-on policy, meaning anyone who wants to train with the team is welcomed. You won't get any financial aid, but you can work and try to make the team."

Sagle corresponded with Bill Dellinger, Bowerman's assistant coach. I received a late academic acceptance; Dellinger said he wanted to meet with me when I arrived.

Wrapping up my senior year, I went back to Germany for the

track championships, won again, breaking my previous record with a 1:55.2 clocking. I was buoyed with new confidence. And was excited about making a move which, for the first time, wasn't the military's idea or my dad's, but mine.

I was headed for the University of Oregon.

Chapter 2
Running Amid Royalty

When I arrived in Eugene in September 1971, I felt more like tourist than resident. True, I understood the environment I was about to enter. In addition to the *Sports Illustrated* issue with Prefontaine on the cover, I had read about Bowerman's coaching, and read *Track & Field News* every month. I paid particular attention to Oregon athletes because I now knew—with Jim Sagle's direction—that UO had a history of developing great distance runners.

In high school, my senior-year term paper had been about Jim Ryun, my hero, the world record holder in the mile. He had since moved from Kansas to Eugene to train for the 1972 Olympics in Munich. But, as I said, it was as if I'd arrived in Eugene not to be part of what was becoming known as "Track Town USA" but to revel in it as an outsider who was now looking in. A fan. Or a wannabe who, unlike the other stud runners from across the country, was here because Bill Bowerman and his assistant, Bill Dellinger, actually wanted them here.

Near as I could tell, the only person who really wanted me here was me.

Once I'd found my Dunn Hall dorm and unpacked, I headed out on campus to take some photos to send back to my parents. Not only did I feel like a tourist, I was acting like one. The Oregon basketball team played in McArthur Court, an aging, ivy-clad arena that dated to 1926. Next to "Mac Court," I discovered, were the shoe-box-sized offices of all the university's athletic coaches, including the man I was supposed to check in with, Dellinger.

Like seemingly every other person connected to UO track and field, Dellinger was a local legend. Thirty-seven, he'd grown up in Springfield, Eugene's blue-collar cousin to the east, and had set all sorts of distance-running records at Oregon; competed in three Olympics (1956, 1960, and 1964); and won a bronze medal in the 5000-meters in Tokyo (1964). He'd become UO's cross-country coach in 1969, the year Prefontaine arrived, and had just become the assistant track and field coach.

His door was open. Dellinger, it turned out, wasn't alone. He'd been chatting with three others, two of whom I'd seen in magazines and newspapers. I tried not to gawk but it was like a folk-music fan suddenly seeing Bob Dylan and Joan Baez. There sat Prefontaine and Ryun, along with some other guy, a little older, who did not appear to be cut from quite the same athletic cloth as the other two.

"Come in, Mr. Bence," said Dellinger. "You might recognize a couple of these guys. Steve, this is Steve Prefonainte and Jim Ryun." I shook their hands, later wondering if it would be sacrilegious to ever wash mine. "And this is a former Oregon middle-distance runner, Phil Knight, now with Blue Ribbon Sports."

I kept gawking at Pre and Ryun. Dellinger turned to the

others. "This is Steve Bence, an incoming freshman half-miler."

"I've heard about you," Prefontaine said. "From Spain, right?"

"Yeah," I said, momentarily stunned—and flattered—that he'd recognized my name.

We made some small talk. Because I had my camera, I took a picture of the three of them, which is still one of my most cherished, and then excused myself. Frankly, I felt awkward being in the same room with these three legends: Dellinger, Pre, and Ryun. I wondered if the other guy, Knight, felt as privileged as I did.

"Good to meet you and good luck this year," said Ryun.

"Your English is very good," said Prefontaine.

I walked out of the meeting on an are-you-kidding-me? high, wasting no time in writing my folks. I'd just met my new coach, a three-time Olympian, and perhaps the two finest distance runners in America, Pre and Ryun. In person!

The irony was that it was the obscure other guy in that gathering—Knight—who would change my life. Forever.

School officially opened in late September and Bowerman held the first meeting of the incoming freshmen. We gathered in Hayward's East Grandstands and waited for Bill. As we did so, I looked around at what was probably close to fifty freshmen. Almost all of us were walk-ons.

"Which of these guys are on scholarships?" I asked someone who seemed to know his way around.

"Just three," he said, and pointed to middle-distance runner Mark Feig, javelin-thrower Russ Francis, and sprinter/hurdler/pole-vaulter Tinker Hatfield.

Feig was the 1971 top high school miler in the country at 4:05 and from South Eugene High next door. Russ Francis, from Pleasant Hill High, a rural school southeast of Eugene, had set the national high school javelin record and was a decathlete. And Tinker Hatfield, a multi-sport athlete, had single-handedly won the state Class AA Track & Field Championships for tiny Central Linn High in the nearby farm town of Halsey by winning four individual events.

Uncanny. Three national-level athletes who, before college, had lived within half an hour of the UO campus. I was beginning to feel all the more out of place, as if I was not only out of my league, but out of my mind for thinking I could survive in a heat this fast.

Nine names were listed on the depth chart for the 880 with lifetime best times, and I was ninth with my 1:55.2 clocking. The fastest was sophomore Nils Emilsson, from Sweden, 1:49.6, the only one of us under 1:50, which was a national-caliber time. The second-best was junior Mike McClendon, from Texas, a good miler with a best of 1:51.6, two seconds behind Nils. The others were in the range of 1:51 to 1:53, including junior Dave Weiker from Canada, freshman Paul Osburn from Seattle, senior Wes Smylie from Tacoma, and the miler, Feig.

Obviously, I was a small fish in a pond that seemed the size of the Pacific Ocean, an hour west.

Suddenly, there was Bowerman standing in front of us. I had heard of him and seen pictures of him. I knew he was a great coach, had earned great respect, and, weirdly, was a prankster. But this was different. This was Bowerman in person—as my coach. He had just turned sixty that year.

When I first saw him, I thought of my grandfather, who was about the same age. My grandfather immigrated to the US from Hungary and worked hard with his hands.

"Let me see those hands," Grandpa would say to my brother, Randy, and me. "Too soft; you need to work harder."

If he saw a bit of a callous on our palms he would rub it. "This is much better."

Grandpa would have liked Bill. But Bill was different. He didn't seem old like my grandfather had. He was alert, sharp, articulate, wise, and athletic in appearance. And—oh, yeah— in a place seemingly wall-to-wall with legendary coaches and athletes, Bowerman was God.

He'd coached in four different decades, replacing the stadium's namesake, Bill Hayward, in 1949. (Hayward had been a legend, too, coaching four world-record holders, six American-record holders, and nine Olympians in his 44-year track and field career at Oregon.) Bowerman replaced Hayward shortly after returning from Italy where, during World War II, he'd emerged as a life-saving hero as part of the heralded 10th Mountain Division.

"Look around you," he said, as if he'd heard the same speech before the 10th Mountain had engaged the Germans at Italy's Brenner Pass. "By the time you freshmen are seniors, only three of you will still be on this team. Some of you will quit because you aren't good enough, some because you aren't tough enough, some because you don't care enough.

"Gentlemen, whether you remain on this team or not, do yourself a favor and take advantage of the opportunity here at Oregon to get a good education."

His eyes swept back and forth like one of those Rain Bird sprinklers, as if not only his words but his gaze could nourish something deep within us, could water our very souls.

"You can only do two things well here at Oregon," he said. "Make one of those your role as a student—because if you don't, you're going to flunk out and spend the rest of your life picking beans or bar fights. Your second choice will come down to your being either a good athlete or a good lover. Pick one."

A few heads went down. I glanced left and right to see the ones who didn't like the limited options, as if they secretly hoped they might be capable of doing three things well. But his voice jolted us out of dwelling too much on such bunny trails.

"Men of Oregon," he boomed. "I invite you to become students of your events. Running, one might say, is basically an absurd pastime upon which to be exhausting ourselves. But if you can find meaning in the kind of running you have to do to stay on this team, chances are you will be able to find meaning in another absurd pastime: life."

Short and sweet. And, frankly, inspirational. He was talking about our higher purpose. I liked the guy, even if he leaned to the limited-options side of things regarding what we could do well. It seemed I needed to focus on two things for the next four years and see where they might lead me.

"And one more thing," Bowerman said. I waited for a cymbal clash of inspiration. "Don't forget to write your mothers."

Formal practices began, and I joined with my fellow half-milers. Bowerman had turned over coaching of the runners to Dellinger. Every Monday morning on my way to class, I'd swing by the locker room to see the training schedule Bill D. had stuck on the bulletin board There was a routine to our training, a rhythm, a purpose that had been finely honed by Dellinger; in high school, my workouts had never been nearly so precisely customized for me.

Dellinger had us do easy workouts for the first two weeks and then threw in a challenging Tuesday workout on the third. We did 2x3 laps, 2x2 laps, 2x1 lap, and 2x½ lap. As the youngest freshman, I couldn't quite hit the target pace and was a little behind the leaders, teetering on discouragement.

One afternoon, after practice, Dellinger came up to me.

"Bence," he said, "you look strong"—I was mentally floating, having been praised by an Olympian—"but your butt sticks out like a logging truck that's losing its load. Tilt your pelvis more underneath, OK?"

"Right, coach."

I had no clue what he meant, but I'd figure it out and do it.

"By the way," he said, "Bowerman wants a word with you."

It was like having been requested to meet with the Pope himself. Heart racing—and not because of my workout—I jogged over to see the man.

"Bence, we're going to see if you can run something other

than two laps," he said. "I'm giving you the first four lessons of hurdling."

Uh-oh. Running was hard enough without putting obstacles in the way. Plus my high school sports experience proved to me that I was only good at left-right-left-right with gradual turns to the left. But Bowerman apparently saw potential in me as a 440-yard intermediate hurdler.

He had three hurdles spaced out on the track and asked me to hurdle them. I ran up to the first hurdle and jumped, took a random number of steps to the second hurdle and jumped again, then a third time. None of it felt the least bit natural.

He began coaching me, taking me through the proper form, the importance of the right number of steps between barriers, and the need to attack each hurdle. He had me run in the lane next to the hurdles, taking five steps between each, and mimicking that I was hurdling. When he thought that I was ready, he had me try it again for real.

I did better but not great.

"Try it again."

My third attempt was going even better until I caught a spike in the track and I fell flat on my face. I bounced up quickly, eager for an evaluation from Bowerman, who gave me one.

"Go back to Dellinger," he said. "You'd better be a good half-miler."

In early November, Bowerman approached me in the locker room as I was getting ready for my Wednesday afternoon run.

"Bence, what are you running today?" he all but yelled over the din of the noisy locker room.

"An easy six, by myself," I yelled back.

"You're a size 9, right?"

"Yes," I said, unsure where he was going with this but happy that he thought me worthy of attention. He handed me a pair of shoes, the likes of which I'd never seen. Growing up, I never paid much attention to the shoes I wore. Few runners did. We called them tennis shoes or sneakers. But these looked and felt special, made specifically for running.

"Wear these test shoes on your run and let me know what you think when you get back."

It wasn't a question, it was a command. But realizing I'd apparently joined a select group of athletes in whom Bill trusted enough to test his ever-evolving experimental shoes, I ran with a bit more bounce in my step that day. Until, that is, about a mile and a half into the run, when my ankle started to seriously hurt. The timing sucked. Bowerman has me test-run his shoes. I tweek an ankle. Either way, this looks like a no-win for me

I finished my six miles with a slight limp and went to see the trainer. He checked out my leg, asked a few questions, then eyed my shoes with a touch of suspicion.

"Let me see the shoes you were wearing."

He looked at them with contempt, shaking his head sideways. "These shoes are crap. The padding under the heel isn't built up. They have a negative heel. Each step is putting an additional strain on your calf and Achilles. Where did you get these disasters?"

"Bowerman," I said. "He gave them to me today to test."

He winced. "You need to give these shoes back to him and tell him that you should never test a pair again. Your track career is way more important than testing out his crazy shoe ideas."

He gave me a new pair of shoes with proper padding. I needed almost a week to heal—in a physical therapy process that included Whirlpool soaks, heat, and ice. Back to normal, I worked up the courage to return the test shoes to Bowerman.

"So, what did you think?" he asked.

"I had an injury that took a week to heal. The trainer thinks it was the shoes—and doesn't want me to test anymore."

"Where did it hurt?"

"In my ankle, calf, Achilles area."

"Good! That's what I thought would happen!"

He happily walked away.

What the—? Was Bowerman a mad scientist who was OK with failure as long as he was learning from it? Or was he testing me, a freshman, in some way to see what I was made of? I eventually surmised it was a little of both.

A week later Bowerman approached me again with a pair of shoes, but asked me to run only a lap in them. I looked at the shoes as someone who was wiser than he'd been before. I liked them. They were comfortable, light, and I thought they'd make a good training shoe. I noted that they were from a Japanese company. Only later would I realize they were a prototype leading to the launch of an upstart running-shoe company he was planning to start with the guy who'd been in Dellinger's office with Prefontaine and Ryun that day: Phil Knight.

Hmm, I thought, maybe he's onto something here.

Chapter 3
1972

After the bleak Oregon winter—Oregonians don't tan, they rust, went the joke—our first spring track and field meet was bathed in the sunshine of California's Fresno State University. As he often did in workouts, the more seasoned Nils Emilsson took charge of the strategy for the 880-yard race.

"Weiker, you take the lead for the first 220 yards. Bence, you take the second 220. I'll take the third. And then it's everyone for themselves."

The wind was a steady 10+ mph with regular gusts. It would be tough to run into the wind, and whoever was in the front would be blocking it for the rest. We didn't expect a fast time.

As planned, Weiker took the lead and I ran right behind him, positioning myself to pass at the 220 mark. Unexpectedly, a Fresno State runner pulled up to my right, just off Weiker's shoulder. I was boxed in and couldn't take the lead as planned.

Weiker had to lead through the entire first lap and then more than half of the second lap because Nils couldn't get around. In the final turn, with 165 yards left, Mike McClendon shot past us, followed closely by Nils, our best and second-best half milers. I was even more boxed in than before, with everyone now jockeying for the win.

The Fresno State runner faded, which opened up space for me. I burst to the outside, quickly caught Nils, then Mike, winning in 1:52.3.

I was happily stunned. Weiker was royally pissed.

"What the hell happened to the plan?" he growled. "You leeched off me for most of the race, and then you find the energy at the very end to pass me?"

It was a big lesson for me. Winning is important, but how you win matters even more, especially with my teammates. I hadn't taken the lead when I'd promised. Win as a team. It's a lesson that would become bedrock stuff years hence when I went to work for Nike.

At Bakersfield the next week—we stayed in California to train in the warm weather—I won again, in 1:52.0, a new PR. But this time I, along with Nils, pissed off Dellinger, who thought we'd dogged the opening lap. Pre, on the other hand, was his usual hard-charging self. He won the 6-mile in 27:22.3, breaking the Oregon and NCAA records.

The next week was my first chance to compete at hallowed Hayward Field. My Dunn Hall dorm was kitty-corner from the track so I put on my gear in my room, grabbed my spikes, and jogged across the street. I entered the stadium as I often did for track practice, but this time was different. There were more than 5,000 people in the stands. I'd never run in front of more than 100 people, and those were mainly other competitors and family members. I felt a rush of andrenalin. I was stoked! And it showed in how I raced.

I won the half-mile by almost two seconds, 1:49.2, my first

sub 1:50. Before I could even get my sweats back on, Wade Bell, a Duck alum and a 1968 Olympian in the 800 meters, came up to talk. So did a couple of reporters. I wasn't used to this kind of attention—not that I minded.

I jogged a little to warm down and then went into the stands to watch the rest of the meet, feeling excited and relieved that I had come through with my third straight win.

Dellinger found me. "Remember last fall how I told you to tilt your pelvis more underneath?"

"Yeah."

"Forget it. Your mechanics are working just fine for you."

The headline in the Sunday *Register-Guard* sports page said, "Rookie Bence breaks 1:50 in home debut."

This was fun.

The next week, in miserable conditions in Seattle—cold and wet—I won again (1:50.8). Afterward, Pre came up to me.

"Bencie, you ran tough today."

"You, too." He'd survived biting winds and massive puddles to win the mile in 4:07, slower than his best high school time, 4:06, but an accomplishment in that godawful weather.

The bus wouldn't arrive back in Eugene until about 10 p.m.

"So what are you planning to do when we get back?" Pre asked.

"Sleep."

"You can't do that. You need to celebrate. We need to celebrate!"

"Got a couple beers chilling in a bag outside my dorm window," I said.

"You can't do that either. It's Saturday night. Meet me at this party on University Street."

It was track season. I was trying to be disciplined. But Pre was insistent—and, hey, it was *Pre*—so I dropped off my gear and found the house. Pre was there, the center of attention, and he gave me a thumbs up that I'd made it. But I didn't stay long and was in bed before midnight.

In Lincoln, Nebraska—there for a dual meet on the Cornhuskers' new tartan-surface track—we changed in the Nebraska locker room. To get to the track we had to walk by the football stadium, where some 50,000 fans were gathering to watch the Huskers' spring game that was starting soon. We'd draw only a smidgen of that.

"Hey, are you the famous Steve Prefontaine?" asked one of the players to Pre.

"Yeah," Steve said.

"Well, look, you're not in Oregon anymore, you're in Nebraska. See that? Our stands are packed—and it's just a practice. You'll be lucky if you have a thousand at your track meet."

This was our welcome to Nebraska? We kept walking. No sense rumbling with a couple of 250-pound guys in full battle gear, especially before a meet.

My race began. On the final curve, I was leading when I heard footsteps. Teammate McClendon pulled even and was trying to pass me. We ran side-by-side but I had enough to win by a step, 1:49.4 to 1:49.5.

In the following week's Twilight Meet, back in Eugene, I outleaned teammate Paul Wilkinson, an intermediate hurdler, to win a special 600-yard race that Dellinger threw in to challenge the two of us. We had identical times of 1:09.9. Six races, six wins.

My expected dual with Ebba of Oregon State the next week never happened because he ran the mile instead—not that I knew until shortly before my race. I'd never been more psyched for an event.

A crowd of 10,000 was anticipated in Eugene and the meet would be carried live on both radio and television. An Oregon-Oregon State dual track and field meet in the 1970s had an almost football-game feel to it. The Pac-8 was the country's premiere track and field conference and we were two of the best programs. It was a different time. Track and field stars would routinely make the cover of *Sports Illustrated*. ABC's "Wide World of Sports" would feature national competitions. I was just honored to be part of it.

Frankly, I didn't think I had much of a chance against Ebba, but I was still pumped for a chance to take him on. Not to brag, but I was fearless.

I was warming up on the intramural track when I heard the guy on the loudspeaker say, "Pre in the lead, Hailu second … ."

What? Hailu's running the 1500 meters? I dashed over to the track and witnessed the end of the race, one of Pre's greatest. It was a race that he should have lost. Three times, Ebba tried to surge by Pre in the final lap. Three times Pre rebuffed him, barely winning in a personal-best 3:39.8. He simply willed himself to win.

As thrilled as I was for him, I was crushed that I wouldn't get a shot at Ebba. When my race began, I felt as if I was going through the motions. No one wanted the lead so I took it, passing the 400 in a slow 56 seconds. OSU's John Svoboda challenged me on the backstretch but I wouldn't let him pass. UO's McClendon came on strong at the end but was trapped by Smylie and me. It was an Oregon 1-2-3 sweep with me winning in 1:49.8, Smylie second in 1:49.9, and McClendon third in 1:50.0.

A week later in the Northern Division race in Corvallis, OSU senior Pat Collins—the 1970 NCAA half-mile runnerup and a guy I'd never heard of—was returning after a couple of injury-plagued years. I would be his first test.

I'd never experienced such a cat-and-mouse game of tactics, initiated by him not me. I tried to pass him going into the second curve; he forced me to run wide to the outside—made my race longer. When we hit the main straight, he slowed. I thought he was tiring, so I moved to the outside to pass him. But he accelerated, forcing me to stay in Lane 2. I was a stride ahead of him, but I couldn't cut in. I slowed to drop in behind him for the third curve, but he slowed again. I couldn't find my way back to the inside lane.

The uneven pace and unexpected game-playing were exhausting, so I eased up on the backstretch. Going into the final turn Collins forged ahead and I found myself in second again. I gave it everything I had in the final stretch but couldn't get by him. He beat me, 1:49.5 to 1:49.7.

"Were you trying to keep me outside?" I asked him afterward.

"Of course."

Slowly, I was learning how this collegiate running race needed to be run; there were tactics, and the seasoned senior just out-smarted the naïve freshman. An article in *The Register-Guard* the next day was headlined, "Pat Collins is back—and Bence is the victim." My seven-race win streak was over. How would I respond?

The Pac-8 Championships were the next week at Stanford. In Friday's 880 heats, in which the top four would qualify for Saturday's finals, I started easy; winning wasn't the goal, and others were forced to the front. Everything was fine until I realized that, with 200 yards to go, I wasn't in the top four and I was once again boxed in.

OSU's Svoboda yelled, "C'mon Bence, move!"

"Can't! Boxed in!"

John sped up, a gap opened, and I got free to finish second. In the process, John got cut off. He finished fifth in the heat, not advancing to the finals. It didn't seem fair: he'd helped me make it and wound up not making it himself.

"Thanks, man," I said afterward. "Sorry you didn't make it."

He shrugged. It was among the most good-hearted things I've ever seen a competitor do—a guy from our archrival, Oregon State, helping me out, apparently in the interest of state-of-Oregon pride.

In Saturday's finals, Collins wanted a fast pace, not the tactical race he had run against me the week before, so passed me and UCLA's Rico Sanchez to take the lead. I followed him, hitting 53.5 for the first lap. Collins pushed the pace through the curve. I loved it; we were racing, just the two of us, ahead of the pack, I matching his increased speed. Then, bang, with 300 yards to go, Cal's Rick Brown—the defending champ—flew by us in a different gear. I responded by passing Collins, hoping that Brown had started his final kick too soon. In the final straight I started to close the gap on him, but he was too far ahead. The Cal runner was first in 1:47.7; I was second in a personal-best 1:48.6, a new freshman school record—and far ahead of fourth-place Nathan Burks (1:50.8) of USC. Ripping Burks was satisfying; when I was seeking a school, it was his coach, Vern Wolfe, who'd snubbed me because he didn't think I was in the same class as his half-milers.

Going into the NCAA championships, my 1:48.6 placed me among the top half-milers in the nation. Smylie and McClendon also qualified, so we had three Ducks in the event.

I felt compelled to seek counsel from Bowerman. I mean, it seemed like a waste to be training at the foot of this track and field guru without plumbing the depths of his wisdom.

"Bill," I said, "do you have any advice for me this week?"

"Sure, enjoy yourself. It's your reward for a great season."

The answer, I would come to learn, was vintage Bowerman: just before a race he would never say anything more than what needed saying—and if what he said might catch you by surprise, it never was fluff.

The national meet was at Hayward Field, across the street from my dorm, where I hung out until it was race time. Thursday was the first round of heats. I knew I had to be in the top three to advance but I wanted to conserve as much energy as possible, which meant running in the pack. As in the Pac-8 meet, I wasn't paying close enough attention and again got boxed in, but escaped in time with a strong finish, 1:48.4 for third, in what turned out to be the fastest heat.

Friday, before the semifinals, I found myself unusually nervous. In some ways, maybe I was feeling like I was living on borrowed time, having survived my last two races despite bonehead strategy. Maybe I'd awoken to the fact that I couldn't just show up; this wasn't a bunch of military brats racing for a championship; these were among the best half-milers in America—even the world. In some ways, maybe I'd been like that 15-year-old Olympic gymnast who shines in the Games because she "doesn't know what she doesn't know." She keeps her poise because she's oblivious to failure—or even the possibility of it.

Was my mojo wearing off?

As our semifinal heat was introduced, the encouragement from folks in the stands sounded as if they were reading my mind.

"Run smart, Steve!"

"Don't get boxed, Bence!"

I looked to the stands in acknowledgment, smiled with a thumbs up, and heard a few knowing laughs in return. We understood each other, these fans and me. Oddly, the impromptu exchange relaxed me. I ran most of the race to the outside, stayed out of trouble, and passed a few towards the end to qualify safely in 1:48.9.

I made the NCAA finals—the kid who'd gotten the cold shoulder from a handful of colleges I'd considered attending the previous year. I ran a victory lap, jumping up on occasion, throwing my arms in the air, and gleefully making a fool of myself. The partisan crowd was more than happy to celebrate the achievement with me. These were "Pre's people," yes. But Oregon fans were really everybody's people; they loved Steve, they loved their Ducks, but what they really loved was athletes—runners, field-events competitors, even athletes from rival schools—who gave it their all and succeeded.

After settling down, I left the stadium, and went back to my dorm where everything was business as usual; people were wrapping things up on a Friday afternoon to prepare for the weekend. It was as though nobody knew that just down the street the best collegiate track athletes in the country were competing on a national stage, and one of their Dunn Hall neighbors had just made Saturday's finals! Oh, well, nobody competes in track and field to be in the spotlight, right?

I woke up Saturday morning with an outlandish thought: by day's end I could be the NCAA half-mile champion, the best collegiate 800-meter runner in the country. (Because it was an Olympic year, the NCAA races were done in meters, not yards.) The season had toughened me, especially in terms of tactics and my willingness to not be pushed around by other runners.

Which is good, because the first lap of the finals felt like roller derby; the stakes were high. I was repeatedly pushed, but this time I pushed back. I was learning how to use my hands and get away with it; you had to in order to survive.

My moment of truth came when going into the final turn with all eight of us runners in a tightly bunched knot. I was towards the back and pushed, even lightly punched, my way to the spot where I wanted to run the curve.

Going into the final stretch I planned to move out to Lane 2 for my final kick. Surprise, everyone else had the same idea. It was a crowded sprint for the finish line and Duck fans were loud. This was my third hard race in three days; I couldn't keep pace, but did finish sixth in 1:47.7, a new personal record, behind Tennessee's Willie Thomas, who won in 1:47.1

I was sixth in the nation, only six-tenths of a second behind the national champion. I scored a point for our team! Not bad for an unknown Air Force brat, I figured.

I never asked Bowerman, but I think he was proud of my effort. And I did enjoy myself.

"Do you know you qualified for the Olympic Trials?" Dellinger asked me shortly after the race.

"I did?"

"Yes. And it's right here at Hayward Field. In July."

I hadn't a clue.

I was invited to the Junior National Championships in Denver, a meet for those 19 years-old-and under. I placed a disappointing third, behind the new high school record-holder, Dale Scott of El Cerrito High School in California, and LSU's Bob Smith. I was chosen as an alternate for the United States-Soviet Union junior dual meet in Sacramento. And, yes, the kid who, only fifteen months ago, was running races against less-than-stellar high school competition in the backwaters of Europe found himself in an Olympic Trials qualifying heat with Bowling Green's Dave Wottle, who would emerge as the 1972 Olympic 800-meter champion, best on the planet.

I wish I'd given Wottle a run for his money. Alas, midway through my first qualifying heat I was gassed. I realized that the clock had struck midnight and Cinderella's time at the ball was over. The season had just gone on too long; this six-month stretch was twice as long as my high school seasons. I had nothing left in the tank.

Wottle won the heat. I was a non-qualifying fifth. I was physically shot, mentally shot. After my heat, I went to the trailer to give a urine sample for drug testing. The last two people inside were Ryun and me. I had run a plodding 1:51.0. Ryun, of course, had easily qualified but he would finish fourth in a finals won by Wottle in world-record-tying time (1:44.3), though Jim would make the Olympic team in the 1500.

Athletes, in some ways, are cursed by the "what-have-you-done-for-me-lately?" attitude, often originating within ourselves. Fresh off an Air Force base in Spain, I had won seven straight races as a freshman, finished second in the Pac-8 meet, and placed sixth in the NCAAs. But as I slunk back to my dorm room that night I had an odd feeling, like I had failed.

Dellinger reminded me otherwise. "Hey, Bence," he told me. "Next fall, you'll be on a full scholarship. Tuition, books, room and board—the works. Way to go."

OK, so, maybe I hadn't failed!

Chapter 4
Shoe Time

Shortly before the Olympic Trials, I became an Adidas athlete. I didn't even know there was such a thing. Don't get me wrong; it's not as if the handful of shoe companies in existence were falling over themselves in an attempt to link-up with Steve Bence. The "invite" meant getting free shoes, a common practice and not a violation of the amateur rules.

When I ran under 1:50, a teammate suggested that I write to John Bragg, Adidas' National Track & Field Representative, and introduce myself, which I did. I must have met his criteria for shoes. Soon, I received three pair of shoes: SL-72 training flats, Interval training spikes, and Spider racing spikes.

I was happy to retire my Tigers for the superior German-made spikes. The difference was in the spike plates, probably the German engineering. Also, I now had a pair of training spikes designed specifically for injury prevention, and a pair exclusively for racing.

Bragg stayed in touch, anticipating my shoe needs. "I would appreciate you dropping me a line as to what you will need," he wrote me in a 1972 letter. I had heard stories that the top athletes would get $100 bills stuffed into the toe of the shoe, which I knew crossed the amateur-athlete line; it never happened to me, although I'd always check!

I assumed there was a limit to how many free shoes I could ask for. I didn't test the limit, asking only for what I needed. Bragg sent new models to me for my feedback, which he apparently passed on to the manufacturer in Germany.

I didn't really know Bragg—I never met him in person— and I assumed that Adidas was happy with him as long as they saw Adidas shoes on the feet of the top American athletes. I was proud to be one of those athletes; the only real thing connecting us was my competing in their product.

The other main brand at the time was Puma, also made by a German company, founded by Rudolf Dassler, brother of Adidas founder Adolf Dassler. The brothers were fiercely competitive, trying to outdo each other, which led to product innovations benefitting the athlete.

Runners preferred Adidas; sprinters wanted Puma. I tried to figure out why; perhaps there were technical differences in the shoes, but for sure there were cultural differences among the people competing in them. I found sprinters different than runners: cockier, extroverted, muscular, and tending to walk with a swagger. Runners were often introverted, insecure, skinny, and cerebral.

I only noted one exception to that rule: Steve Prefontaine; that guy was like a sprinter in a runner's body.

American brands included Wilson, Spot-Bilt, the extra-wide New Balance, Saucony, Etonic, and Converse. They were a far cry from the modern track shoes of the time. The American shoes were outdated and stale; the industry didn't seem interested in listening to the athlete. Since I wanted to compete at the elite level, I needed to pick the best, one of the German brands.

The lone Japanese brand was Tiger, the type of shoe that I was wearing before I stepped up to Adidas. At the time, I didn't know much about the shoe landscape. Only later would I learn that Knight had introduced Tiger to the US through Blue Ribbon Sports (BRS), the company he founded with Bowerman. He had ordered his first shoes from Japan in 1964, coincidentally the same year of the Tokyo Olympics in which Dellinger had won his bronze medal.

I had been ten years-old in 1964, living in North Canton, Ohio, courtesy—of course—of the Air Force. During the 1956 Olympics (Melbourne) and 1960 Olympics (Rome), I had been in Japan, where I started kindergarten and moved up the elementary-school ladder before Dad was transferred back to the States.

Just a kid, I was obviously unaware of the efforts of Bowerman, Knight, and Jeff Johnson as they made improvements to the Tiger shoes. By the time I was a freshman in college, Tiger had good training shoes, but the competition spikes were not quite ready for prime time; I knew that because I had raced in them.

The timing of the 1972 Olympic Trials—June 29 to July 9—couldn't have been better for BRS to launch the new Nike brand. The top US athletes and diehard fans were coming to Eugene, Nike's home. The competition would be top-notch, with lots of free time for fans to kill, meaning plenty of time for them and competitors to talk, and buy, shoes.

I had been eliminated on the first day of competition, as I said, but word got out that if you came to the BRS store and could prove that you were competing in the Trials, you'd get a free pair of Nike shoes and a tee shirt with your name on the back. It was my first visit to The Athletic Department, in downtown Eugene on 10th and Olive—99 West 10th, Suite 104 to be exact. Sure, I'd love a pair of shoes.

Geoff Hollister was the store manager and, I assumed, the originator of this promotional effort. He had graduated from nearby South Eugene High and run for the Oregon track team in the mid-1960s, lettering as a steeplechaser.

The store was a beehive of activity. Athletes from across the country were trying on shoes, talking shoes, and waiting for the letters to be heat-pressed onto their Nike tees. An assortment of BRS people, even Knight and his wife Penny, were flitting around. They took time to talk about shoes, track and field, and running in general—to anyone interested.

I was surprised that the young clerk, Willie Brock, recognized me and said he'd get me shoes and a tee. He said Wottle had been in the previous day.

"He looked so different off the track," he said. "I told him, 'Hey, you need to wear your hat so we can recognize you.'"

Around town, especially at Hayward Field, I saw athletes wearing the Nike-branded stuff, provoking the question, "What's Nike?" Or in some cases, "Who's Mike'" The new company was getting the name out there and it was working.

"Anyone wearing Nike in competition?" I asked.

"Just some guys in the marathon. Five wore the Moon Shoes hand-made by Geoff—with, of course, Bowerman's direction—but only Mark Covert finished; he was seventh.

I was surprised that five runners would agree to switch shoes just before such a major competition.

I passed on the tee shirt but was given a pair of Nike Wet Flytes, navy blue/white, leather with some kind of coating to give them a perpetual wet-looking shine. I thought it made them look like cheap vinyl shoes. I tried them on, then ran down the street and back.

"What'd ya think?" Hollister asked.

"I wouldn't run in them," I said, taking on some of Pre's brashness. "They're too bulky. Feel heavy, poor cushioning. Plus I don't like the cosmetics. I wouldn't walk around in them."

I couldn't believe how picky I was becoming; was I getting

spoiled?

"Don't tell anyone," said Hollister. "I'll swap you a pair of Leather Cortez. You can try them, and if they're something that you'd run in, they're yours."

I loved them. They reminded me of the prototypes that Bowerman had asked me to run a lap in. I stopped training in my Adidas SL-72 shoes, which became my every-day walk-around shoes. The Leather Cortez became my training shoe of choice. On the track I continued to train in the Adidas Interval and race in the Adidas Spider.

Later, when the Cortez wore out, I went back to Hollister for a replacement pair.

"Sorry," he said, "I can only offer the shoes if you're committed to compete in Nikes, which you aren't, right?"

"Right." I wasn't aware of any Nike spikes beyond the few handmade pairs that Bowerman cobbled together, and I wasn't signing up to be a guinea pig.

I finished my racing career in Adidas. But regarding my training shoes, I ran a thought by Hollister. "Could I trade my new pair of Adidas training shoes for the Leather Cortez?"

"Sure," Geoff said, "I can do that."

It was genius on Geoff's part. For the majority of the time people would see me in Nikes—walking around campus, on a training run, warming up for a race; I would be a walking advertisement for Nikes. But in the short amount of time that I was competing, I would be in Adidas.

In later years, Jeff Johnson, BRS's first full-time employee and a photographer for *Track & Field News*, took tons of pictures of runners at Hayward Field, both in competition and random, including candid shots. When I saw Nike's first catalog, there were two pictures of me, taken by Jeff.

In the Cortez section, I was wearing Nike shoes. I hadn't been paid for allowing my photo to appear in the catalog and hadn't signed a release, but was happy to play a part in the early start-up.

Hey, the fledgling company needed all the help it could get.

The summer of 1972 reminded me that I was living in the epicenter of the world's running universe. Five runners living in Eugene qualified for the US Olympic team: Steve Prefontaine (5000), Kenny Moore (marathon), Mike Manley (steeplechase), Steve Savage (steeplechase), and Cornell's Jon Anderson (10000), who was the son of Eugene Mayor Les Anderson, giving the already-rich Trials an extra scoop of pride for the hometown fans.

In Munich come fall, the distance events were among the highlights of a September-October Olympic Games clouded by a horrific attack by terrorists, who killed ten members of the Israeli team. Poker-faced Wottle—wearing his traditional cap—won gold in what would become a historic 800 meters. He went from worst-to-first on the final lap in what would come to be considered one of the gutsiest comebacks in Olympic history.

Prefontaine (5000) faded to fourth in a balls-to-the-wall race in which he gallantly kicked early and tried desperately to hold a lead, but wasn't able to sustain the pace. Finland's Lasse Viren won. Pre was beyond deflated.

The marathon featured a wild, memorable finish. An imposter, a student, emerged from the tunnel onto the track ahead of Frank Shorter and pretended to be the leader. The ABC television commentary by Erich Segal, author of *Love Story*, was priceless.

"That is an imposter! Get him off the track! This happens in bush league marathons! Throw the bum out! Get rid of that guy! Come on Frank, you won it! It's a fake, Frank!"

Shorter, Moore, and Jack Bachelor went 1-4-9 for the US, the best marathon finish by a single country in the Olympics.

Pre's 5000 and Kenny's marathon overlapped, so neither knew how the other did. When they met up, Pre asked Kenny how he'd done.

"Fourth," said a dejected Moore, who had narrowly missed a medal.

"Fourth?" said Pre. "That's great! Think about it. In 1968 you were 14th. This year, fourth. Fourth in the world! It's a huge accomplishment, you need to be proud!"

"Sure, Pre. How'd you do?"

"Fucking fourth. Is there anything worse than fourth in the Olympics?"

It was vintage Pre, who would be despondent for months. He expected to win that race, ran to win it, and should have at least medaled. But in his effort to win the gold, he was so spent that he was nipped at the finish for third. What looked to be a heroic finish wound up being, in his eyes, a pathetic loss. He was embarrassed, refusing to talk to reporters, though *The Register-Guard's* Blaine Newnham did coax him for some quotes.

Pre rebounded ever so slowly and began focusing on the 1976 Olympics. Back in Eugene, he rejoined us, his teammates, on our normal runs. He returned to his usual cocky self, able to dish it out and take it.

"Hey, did you hear they're going to name a street for me in Coos Bay?" he said as a group of us headed down Hendricks Hill one autumn afternoon in 1972.

"What are they going to call it—Fourth Street?" wisecracked someone from up front.

He chased the guy down Hendricks as if Pre were a runaway truck. That, too, was Pre. He would defend himself on the track—or off. At a 1973 dual meet with Oregon State in Corvallis, an OSU fan with no love for the Ducks was holding court after Hailu Ebba ran a 3:58.1 mile. Pre was running the two-mile later on.

"Pre's lucky he chose the two," said the Beaver. "No way he beats Hailu today. No way!"

Suddenly, from a few rows away: "You're full of shit!"

It was Pre, chilling with some buddies in the stands before

starting his warm-up.

The 1970s were a great time to be a runner. Beyond track and field, road-running was hitting its stride. All-comers races, mostly 10K in distance, became a regular offering. Everyday runners, for the first time, had a chance to compete. Oregon, not surprisingly, was among the hotbeds for such races. And Eugene was at the center of it all. Its "Storm the Butte"—now "Butte to Butte"—began in 1973 and would become one of the longest-held races in the country.

Long before I arrived in Eugene, Bowerman had introduced Eugene and America to jogging on the same Hayward Field track where I now trained. In December 1962, Bowerman, while in New Zealand to coach a UO team that held the world 4x1 mile record, had been invited to "jog" with running guru Arthur Lydiard. Nobody outside of New Zealand had ever heard of this idea—running slowly for health reasons.

Once back in the states, Bowerman started spreading the gospel of jogging to Eugene and the rest of America. With local physicians helping and *The Register-Guard* publicizing, Bowerman invited people to come to Hayward Field on a Sunday afternoon to hear about—and try—this new phenomenon. Two dozen turned out, some women in long coats and street shoes. By the third week, 200 were on hand, the next week more than 2,000. *Life* magazine sent a reporter. The craze had begun.

"Runners in those days were regarded as eccentric at best, subversive and dangerous at worst," wrote Moore for *Sports Illustrated*. "Cars would routinely swerve to try to drive a runner off the road."

But as Bob Dylan sang, "the times they were a changin'." Shorter's 1972 win in the marathon inspired more runners to stretch their distances. Beyond Oregon, road races popped across the country like autumn mushrooms. Everywhere you looked, there were runners.

And every one of those runners needed one thing to do it: shoes.

Chapter 5
Pre's 'Heir,' Bowerman's Wrath

Going into my sophomore year in the fall of 1972, I had to decide where I wanted to live. Pre owned a trailer in Springfield that he shared with another runner, Pat Tyson. Most of my teammates were either living in apartments or fraternities, but I wasn't a frat guy; too many distractions from studying and training.

I found an affordable apartment on Eugene's Mill Street, walking distance from campus, but needed a roommate to share expenses. Dellinger found a solution: Paul Geis, a great 5000-meter runner from Rice who was transferring from the Houston school to Oregon.

"He's looking for a place to live," said Dellinger. "Call him."

In late summer I did so, finding we had a few things in common. As freshmen, we both had run in the NCAA championships, made the USA National Junior team, and run in the Olympic Trials.

"Why are you leaving Rice?" I asked.

"I need to move. I can't make the progress I want in Texas."

He would lose a year of eligibility but could train with the team, compete in open meets, unattached, and compete at the national level as an Oregon Track Club athlete.

Paul OK'd us becoming roommates. When he arrived in late September 1972, we started a routine of running together twice a day, Paul dragging me along on longer distances than I usually ran as a half-miler. He always had to be a half stride ahead of me, so I gave up my usual training-run style—side-by-side—and instead looked straight ahead while talking. Paul was a talker, turning his head as though he wanted to speak face-to-face, but as I said, always slightly in front.

We soon welcomed a roommate, Ron Wayne, a marathoner and grad student who'd just graduated from the University of Massachusetts. Neither of us knew much about him, other than that he needed a placed to live—and, significantly, had a car.

"Sold!" I said. "He's moving in this evening."

Like Paul, he had come to Eugene to run in the Olympic Trials three months earlier—the marathon—and had fallen in love with the place. It's easy to do. Eugene is nestled in the trees of the southern Willamette Valley, features two buttes (Spencer and Skinner) and two rivers (the Willamette and the McKenzie), and is only an hour away from the majestic Cascades Range to the east and the Pacific Ocean to the west. And then, like now, was the running capital of the world.

Ron was a training-machine, logging about 120 miles per week. Each weekday, starting promptly at 6 a.m, he left to run the same 13-mile loop, finishing with an odd breakfast: starting on a loaf of bread that he would gradually eat all day long. On weekeday afternoons, he'd put in an additional seven miles. On weekends, he'd go for a 20-miler just for fun.

Between the three of us, we were respectable in the distances from 440 yards to a marathon, and found plenty of opportunities to train together.

Paul and I soon realized that we were the Odd Couple. I was an introvert, serious about studying; Paul was an extrovert, always looking for a party. He would invite new friends to the apartment, often staying up well past midnight. Gradually, he was pulling me out of my shell, and it was exhausting.

Beyond running, what we had in common was our competitiveness. A pre-med student, he had to take a mandatory fall-term organic chemistry class that he said would "separate those who will become doctors from those who won't." I listened to him all term complain about how tough it was—as though I wouldn't be able to handle it. So, to shut him up, I took the same class winter term. My goal was simple: get a better grade than him. I did so. Paul changed his major to business. I remained a math major, adding some computer science classes—computers were the new thing—that I thought seemed more practical for a post-grad job.

The three of us took turns cooking, two days each per week, and on the seventh day, on discount night, we'd go to an all-you-can-eat buffet. My go-to meal was Hamburger Helper, which I was planning one evening when Paul came into the kitchen.

"Bencie, I bought something new, Rice-A-Roni. Give it a try."

"Why don't you cook it on your day? I know what I'm doing for today."

"You're in a rut. Here, read the instructions on the box."

With his usual intensity, Paul coached me as if I were an Apollo 13 astronaut and he was in mission control trying to get me back to earth after the craft's oxygen tank failed. I took out a pan, took the butter from the refrigerator, and opened the box.

"No, no, no," he said.

I held my tongue.

"That's not right," he said.

He was getting on my nerves.

"You need to sauté the rice!"

Enough.

"You do it!" I shouted as I threw the box at him, rice flying in all directions.

I surprised myself. I guess I could get intense, too. Ron walked into the kitchen to see the last round of the fight. Paul headed out the door to seek refuge with teammate Scott Daggatt.

Perhaps the best way to describe Paul Geis would be in his own words. That year, in an interview with Garry Hill of *Track & Field News*, he said: "I came out to Oregon for the NCAA championships and Olympic Trials and I really dug the running atmosphere. I went back home and I realized that there was no running atmosphere in Houston. Like zero. I just split. It was bad. My father was mad at me, he didn't want me to give up my scholarship at Rice. He took my car away from me. But then he gave me another one, so what the hell."

Clearly, he wasn't afraid to speak his mind, even about Oregon's patron saint of running, Prefontaine.

"I'm really getting sick about all this crap about Pre, like, 'When are you gonna beat him?' Don't make any of those Pre comparisons. I'm so fed up with that bullshit around here. I'm just getting tired of it. 'Pre's a great runner,' everyone says. Don't say great, just say good. He's all right." In Eugene, that was border-line sacrilegious; Pre was everyone's favorite.

Regarding the AAU, which wanted runners like us to make the US proud but did little to support us financially, Geis said: "I really don't want to travel with the AAU. I did that last summer and I was the little bastard on the tour. I really was. A troublemaker."

He wasn't through with the writer, Hill.

"Hey! Are you going to make me look ridiculous in this article? I don't know if you've noticed, but I'm acting really modest and all that. Have you noticed? I'll tell you what. Make me look modest in this article. Why don't you do that? I don't want to come across as an egotistical bastard. Hey, wait a minute, let's get this interview organized. Ask me some straight questions and I'll give you some straight answers."

And with that final sentence, the interview was over. Hill had everything he needed.

Soon it was our turn to throw a party. It seemed simple enough: a keg of beer, a hundred red plastic cups, a few chips, a little word-of-mouth publicity to invitees, a little loud music, and a front door left open. We were ready at 6 p.m. but for the first few hours, hardly anyone showed up. We talked, mainly about track. The party was a complete bomb.

Then he came: Pre. Like the way Top Ramen puffs up when you put it in boiling water, Pre's presence magically expanded—and enlivened—the party. Suddenly our place was packed. Many were on the track team and I realized how little I knew about the sprinters, jumpers, and throwers. Each of the groups normally stuck together and had its own culture; it was nice to intermingle for a change.

I met John Woodman, a freshman hurdler who would become a lifelong friend.

"Call me Woody," he said.

"Where you from?"

"Corvallis."

The home of our rival, Oregon State.

"How'd you end up in Eugene?"

"I decided I wanted to run track in college, and this is the best track school, right?"

"Is your family OK with that?"

"Yeah, my parents are happy for me. The rivalry's not as intense as you might think."

Prefontaine realized the keg was getting low and knew just what to do. He collected a dollar per person, and drove off to buy a pony keg. He returned just in time; the other one had just been drained and, naturally, people were beginning to leave. No beer, no party.

"The beer is here!" Pre announced. Like an onshore breeze from his hometown on the coast, Coos Bay, a second wind infused the party with more energy. Good ol' Pre.

I had a great indoor season, even if it was short: only eight days. I placed second at the Portland Invitational meet in a 1000-yard race that I should have won. On the 165-yard plywood track, with less than two laps to go, I let Washington's Greg Gibson and Oregon State's Clay Lowery pass me. It was a tactical blunder. I wasn't tired at the end, I just wasn't sure of the pace for a distance that I'd only run once before, and didn't push the pace at a critical moment when I had the lead.

With the steeply banked corners that kill momentum, it had been almost impossible for me to pass that late in the race. I got beyond Lowery, but not Gibson, finishing in 2:10.7, a tenth of a second behind the Husky. It was a UO indoor school record.

I found Bowerman to get his permission to run in another indoor meet.

"Bill," I said, perhaps a bit brashly, "I'd like to run in Louisville."

"Maybe, if you can run a 2:08 in Seattle. You shouldn't have let Gibson pass you."

"I know. It was my lack of indoor experience."

"No," Bowerman said, "It was your lack of indoor *intelligence.*"

Someone walked by and said, "Nice race, Steve!"

"It was a stupid race," Bowerman snapped, his eyes fixed, like lazer beams, on the guy who'd given me the compliment. "He looked for his girlfriend in the stands, trying to look good, and didn't pay attention to what he was doing."

I didn't have a girlfriend in the stands, but I understood his message: don't let my mind drift in the middle of a race.

Bowerman was like Oregon's weather: calm and mild most of the time, with an occasional storm that could knock down trees.

Seven days later I won in Seattle, in 2:10.2, breaking my own UO record for 1,000 yards.

Bowerman didn't send me to Louisville. Instead, he retired. I hadn't seen it coming; nobody had. I later assumed that he planned 1972 to be his last track season but because of all that was going on that year—the NCAA Championships and Olympic Trials in Eugene, and his being the head track and field coach for the Olympics—he decided to wait to announce his retirement until just before the 1973 outdoor season.

Bowerman had been the UO head track coach from 1949 to 1972, a total of 24 seasons: six generations—six four-year cycles of athletes. I was a freshman during his final year, the very last of his stellar career. He had a bigger-than-life reputation, but I saw him as a simple down-to-earth man from the small town of Fossil in north-Central Oregon.

I would come to believe that what made Bill special was his ability to solve problems. I could picture him obsessing over finding a solution, fearless in his trial-and-error process, using the resources and people around him, bored if he woke up in the morning without a list of problems to solve.

People called Bill an innovator, which he was; he's in the Inventor's Hall of Fame. But Tom, one of three Bowerman sons, told me that Bill wouldn't know what that word means. Bill didn't wake up in the morning asking himself, "How can I innovate today?" But he would wake up thinking about the problems he wanted to solve, and in his quest, the innovations followed. And so he was able to overcome whatever he faced.

Our first competition of the outdoor season was an intrasquad meet that included Oregon Track Club athletes, meaning Geis was eligible, and would be open to the public. The Friday *Register-Guard* reported that I would move up, and Geis down, to the mile. Bragging rights in our apartment were on the line. Never mind that there was another fairly decent runner entered in the mile who had the potential to blow both of us out of the water: Pre. To date, he'd lost only two races at Hayward Field.

Although the format was informal—most competitors just wore workout gear—Geis and I decided it would be a great opportunity to wear our USA uniforms, even if it was a hot dog move. We rationalized that it would give us added incentive.

"Now we need to run well," I said. "We can't wear the USA singlet and finish in the back of the pack."

Pre and Geis led us through laps of 60, 62, and 63. We reached the three-quarter mile mark in 3:05, the three of us closely bunched with a lap to go. The pace was perfect for me. With about 165 yards to go, I shifted into my half-mile speed to pass Pre, and then Geis, winning in 4:05.5.

I mainly cared about beating Geis, my roommate, but I had beaten Prefontaine—by more than a second. He was third in 4:06.6.

But some context, unfortunately for me, is in order. Dellinger and Bowerman wanted Pre to go an additional lap that day—do 2000 meters. He did so, listed in the next day's paper as the lone entry—and the winner—of that event. He was also listed as having finished third in the mile, behind me. I've always felt—wink, wink—that I was robbed of my moment in the sun that day; yeah, I'd beaten Pre, but the race would always have an asterisk next to it.

As a sophomore, I ran in eight races before heading into the Pac-8 Championships in Eugene. My two losses were to UCLA's Tony Veney by 0.2 seconds and to WSU's Dale Scott by 0.3. I also hadn't met the 1:49.5 standard for the NCAA meet, coming up just 0.1 seconds short. To qualify, I looked forward to the Pac-8 Championships at Hayward Field.

Then disaster struck. Two days before the meet, Dellinger wanted me to run several quick 165-yard sprints. It was a warm day; I told Bill that my left thigh felt strange. Bill had me warm up a little extra. On my first 165, my leg cramped. There was a sharp pain in my thigh, which felt strained or pulled, I didn't know which. I fell to the track.

Dellinger rushed to me, feeling guilty I later assumed, for having not been more cautious with me. He surmised that I was short on salt and sent me to the training room for treatment.

"Steve," he told me later, after conferring with the team trainer, "I think we need to hold you out of the Pac-8 meet."

"But I need that meet to qualify for nationals."

"And your body simply isn't ready to run a qualifying half-mile and then a final."

"But Bill, I—."

"Bence, the meet's only two days away."

I let it go at that, but wrestled with his decision through most of a sleepless night; each year, the NCAA Championships was the meet I wanted to peak for. The next morning, shortly before Bill had to turn in our final roster for the meet, I poked my head into his cubbyhole office next to Mac Court.

"Bill, it's feeling better. Honest. With two days of treatment, I can be ready."

He rolled his eyes and looked away.

"I can score points for us."

I'd hit him in the only place I knew I could connect.

"Get to the trainer—now. I want the works: electrical stimulation, heat, salt, muscle relaxers, aspirin, massage."

"Got it, Bill! Thanks."

The two days of treatment worked. I ran. I breezed through Friday's semifinal; the top four in each heat would advance to the finals. My normal quick start was painful so I slowed, ran safely, finished fourth, and advanced. I didn't hit the NCAA's qualifying standard so would have to run a fast race in the finals.

By Saturday, I felt confident that I could run well, though I wasn't as confident that I could handle a fast finish. To compensate, I decided to start faster than normal, then try to hold on to the end. The first lap felt good, a lightning-fast 52 seconds. I was leading. The treatment seemed to have paid off.

I quickly did the math; another 52-second lap would give me a 1:44, a world record. Ha! That wasn't going to happen, but I needed at least a 57.5-second final lap—and thought I had that in me. With roughly half a lap to go, I was still leading. Then, bang, for the second year in a row Cal's Rick Brown blew by me. I knew he was in a different league than me. Nevertheless, my competitive instincts kicked in. Without thinking, I went with him.

Coming down the final straight, Brown was well ahead. I saw the finish line, and heard the roar of the Hayward Field crowd amp to another level; our fans were unbelievably smart. They knew I needed an impressive finish to qualify.

Zap. I hit the wall. It had never happened to me before. I didn't gradually slow down; instead, in a single step my legs went to rubber. I was like an F-14 getting shot out of the sky. I'd never experienced anything like this in a race. What was I to do? Grab my leg and fake a severe injury? Step onto the infield and quit?

I decided to finish; if I could stay in the top six I'd at least score a point, my promise to Dellinger. But I couldn't do it. In an instant, the whole field lumbered past me. I finished seventh in 1:50.7.

No team points. No qualifying time. No more races to run. My season was over. Or was it?

The next day, Dellinger and Oregon State Coach Berny Wagner—both had athletes desperate for NCAA qualifying marks—did some brainstorming. When they were finished, they had set up a special Twilight meet in Eugene, on a Tuesday evening, to replace the outdated Northern Division meet. I suddenly had one more opportunity to run under 1:49.5.

OSU's Ebba, who'd already qualified in the mile and would

place fourth in the NCAA Championships, was going to run the half-mile just for training purposes. We talked beforehand. His hip was sore; he wasn't even sure he could finish, but committed—without my even asking—to help me get the necessary time.

I felt great. My leg seemed healed. I ran in second place for the first lap, pulled along by OSU's Noel Rix.

"Fifty-four!" yelled the timer at the end of the first lap. Perfect.

I took the lead, Ebba on my heels. He pulled alongside me in the final turn, pushing the pace. I responded in like manner. As if knowing his job was done, Ebba fell back. I surged down the homestretch, the sound of the crowd—yes even impromptu meets drew decent crowds in Eugene—surging, too. I pushed harder. Hang on. Hang on. I desperately needed 1:49.4 or better. I hit the tape.

In seconds I heard it: "You qualified!" someone yelled.

I was ecstatic.

"It's in the 1:48s," someone said.

I threw my arms into the air and started my victory lap, my smile stretching wide.

The loudspeaker cracked on. "Officially, it's 1:48.2 for Bence, who qualifies for the NCAA meet!"

I sped up my victory lap, waving my arms to the crowd, and jumped as awkwardly as I had the year before at the NCAA semifinal. I was getting a standing ovation. Dellinger caught up, put his arm around me and shook my hand for the newspaper cameras.

I was going to Baton Rouge with the fifth-fastest time in the nation. My season wasn't over after all!

Only 19 half-milers—usually there are about 25—qualified for the nationals, so we didn't need to run a first round. In the semifinals I finished third, in a lifetime best of 1:48.1, the equivalent of 1:47.4 for 800 meters. I advanced to the finals.

The final race Saturday was scheduled for 4:35 p.m., live on national television. My parents, now in Ohio, were watching. I warmed up with my normal routine, but at 4:20 p.m., fifteen minutes early, we were summoned to the starting line. I rushed to take off my sweats and tie my shoes. The starter said to relax, there were still seven minutes to go.

"What's going on?" I asked.

"TV commercials and an update on golf."

I did a double-take on who it was I was talking to. My gosh, it was O.J. Simpson, in person, on the track nearly in front of me, wearing headphones—the NFL football great and former USC football and track standout. He had called us early to be sure the race would start at the exact time needed for television. I liked that we were on TV, but I was pissed. We were about ready to race for the national championship crown, and we were standing around waiting.

Simpson gave the starter a signal for two minutes, then 1:40, then a countdown from 20 seconds. The starting gun sounded.

I started in Lane 2, and settled into second place, exactly where I wanted to be for the first half lap, complete with the shoving that I had learned to handle. At the end of the first lap, I was still in second although I was more into Lane 2 than I wanted. I imagined my parents yelling at the TV with a lap to go.

But with a half lap left I was hurting, and faded from second to sixth, with Cal's Brown nipping me at the finish to place fifth. I matched my freshman result, sixth in the nation, in 1:48.5 for 880 yards, basically the same time for 800 meters the year before.

Four of us scored points for the team—Pre (3 mile), Mac Wilkins (discus, shot put), Craig Brigham (decathlon), and me (880). Our total of 31 points placed us second as a team behind UCLA.

Would I like to have finished higher than my freshman

year? Sure. But given that ten days before I was sprawled on the track after freezing up during that 165, how could I complain?

Thanks to a helluva trainer, to Dellinger and Wagner for throwing together the last-minute meet, and to Ebba for having pulled me to my qualifying time, I'd placed in the nationals once again.

I was good with that.

Chapter 6
Pre, Mary, and The Great Race

After the 1973 track season, Mark Feig approached me to be roommates for our junior year. I think it was actually the idea of his father, Myron. Mr. Feig was a huge track supporter and manager of Carl Greve Jewelers in Eugene. He thought it would be best for us two middle-distances runners to room together. Fine by me.

Mark, then at South Eugene, had been the fastest high school miler in the country his senior year, 1971, with a 4:05 clocking. He was outgoing and more connected with the distance runners, especially Pre, so drew me deeper into that circle.

As nice a guy as he was, Feig wasn't the most important person I met that year. That would be a girl named Mary Jacko, who I met on a blind date. A teammate, Scott Dahlberg, was dating Mindy Meserve, a Kappa Alpha Theta sorority girl, who had a friend who he thought might be a good fit for me. Turns out he was right.

We decided it would be a double date, plus Mark, at our apartment, with Mark and me making the best meal we could. In other words, nobody should arrive with great expectations. But meeting Mary was far better than tasting the pork chops and mashed potatoes that we served.

After our first date, Mark was convinced Mary was perfect for me.

"Don't let her get away, Bencie," he said.

He started introducing her with a "this-is-Steve's-girlfriend" line, as if his believing deeply enough would somehow make it come true.

"Man, I hardly know her," I told him.

"She's the one. Don't blow it."

Once I'd accepted that she was my steady girlfriend, Mark upped the ante.

"This is Steve's fiancé," he started saying when introducing her.

It was only a matter of time until he would introduce her as "Steve's wife," which, ultimately, would be accurate. But, then, I'm getting ahead of myself.

As a junior, I once again failed to run an NCAA qualifying time during the regular season and it came down to the finals of the Pac-8 Championships in the LA Coliseum. I was healthy, ran conservatively the first lap in fifth place, and when Cal's Brown passed me, just as he'd done the previous two years, I followed. We passed runners one at a time. With 100 yards to go, we passed USC's James Baxter and we were leading the field. I made a charge at Brown but finished second once again with an NCAA qualifying time of 1:48.4. Brown was doubled over, not able to jog for a few minutes. He wanted the win badly but I'd given him a race. It was his fourth Pac-8 title.

The 1974 NCAA Championships were in Austin. The whole team competed poorly in the heat and humidity. I didn't advance beyond the first round, in part because I had a fever. Dellinger knew something was wrong and sent me to see the trainer. It was a dark day for Oregon track and field with studs Pre and Mac Wilkins having graduated. We scored only 10 points, all coming from Geis, the new national champion in the 5000. Being from Houston, he wasn't bothered a bit by the heat.

Beyond the college scene, a quiet discontent was brewing among many any amateur track and field athletes in the early '70s. At issue were the leaders of track and field organizations, mainly the AAU, making money on the backs of amateurs—while forbidding the athletes from capitalizing on their skills. Prefontaine was among the first to challenge the system—and by far the most visible.

Pre had done OK financially when he was in school and on a full scholarship, but things got tough after his graduation. As far as I knew, this was the first year that the AAU began prohibiting track athletes from competing internationally during certain times of the summer. They wanted to force US athletes to compete in the AAU Championships and in its dual meet that pitted the US against the USSR. The AAU wanted the biggest American stars all to itself but offered no compensation, even though the organization would benefit.

Not only did Pre plan to skip the AAU Championships, he told the world as much—with the usual Pre bravado.

"I'm going to compete all through their moratorium and if they want to take me to court, that's fine with me," Prefontaine told Track & Field News. "I can take them for all they're worth. What does it prove, running the AAU meet? The AAU doesn't care about the athletes; why should I care about them?"

The AAU wasn't listening. It offered no help with the costs of training, competition, and living. Prefontaine was internationally famous—a reputation he solidified in college—but to be able to keep training, he was all but forced to take race money under the table.

Meanwhile, he was offered $200,000 to turn pro. He turned it down. Had he taken the money, he would have lost his amateur status and his eligibility to compete in the 1976 Olympics.

In spring 1974, Pre encouraged a handful of former teammates to join him in Europe for the summer, assuring us that we could show up, enter meets, and get paid—just as he had done the previous summer. I was intrigued by the idea of extending my junior 800-meter season and having a European summer adventure. Along with seven or eight others, I took him up on the offer. Feig and I spent nearly two months running 16 races in Sweden and Finland, negotiating payment with meet directors, and pocketing the money.

After expenses, I made $133. Then I ran for Oregon my senior year, which technically compromised my amateur status. I'd broken the rules, the NCAA's and the AAU's. But I never regretted it in the least, because as time and the courts ultimately proved, the rules were patently unfair. Congress would pass the Amateur Sports Act of 1978, providing legal protection for individual athletes, removing the AAU as the governing body, and vindicating Pre in his fight against the amateur rules at the time.

Meanwhile, I returned to the US on August 7, 1974, having won four of the eleven 800s I ran, my fastest time a fourth place (1:47.3) in Stockholm behind the US's Rick Wohlhuter, who nearly broke the world record that night. I was exhilarated not only by my results but by joining Pre in his fight. Even though we were, in the eyes of the sports establishment, wrong, remember: this was the coming of a new generation. If reason wouldn't change the rules, we were willing to break those rules until people wised up. I suppose that made me a rebel.

The fall of my senior year arrived, and with it one of the most obscure—but fascinating—chapters of the Steve Prefontaine story. "The Great Race" was an annual Oregon-vs.-Oregon State fraternity fundraiser for Muscular Dystrophy. Runners ran from Corvallis to Eugene in odd-numbered years and from Eugene to Corvallis in even-numbered years.

In November 1974 the event was set to finish at OSU's Parker Stadium during halftime of the Civil War football game— back when it could be called that. In order to accomplish this, all but the last four miles were to be run on Friday, with the race resuming during the second quarter of the game.

A friend in a fraternity asked if I would run on the Oregon team. I agreed because the race included way more than the AAU ever gave us: a few hours on a bus with sorority girls and beer. It wasn't a serious race; even if Oregon and Oregon State were rival schools, the Beavers had more than earned my respect with the way two of their runners—Svoboda and Ebba—had helped me in qualifying races. It was just a fun Friday-Saturday event for a good cause. There weren't many rules and we could decide, as the race progressed, who would run, in which order, and how far. Plus, at the end, we could see the end of the game.

On Friday, on the bus, people started to party as they completed their runs. However, I turned competitive after the Oregon State team pulled ahead and its bus disappeared into the distance, three or four minutes ahead of us.

Unacceptable. I worked out a two-part plan. For the remainder of Friday's segment, instead of guys running one or two miles at a time, we started running about a quarter mile at a time.

"We can dramatically increase our pace each time," I said to my teammates. "The Beavs won't know what hit them."

It worked. The Oregon State bus came back into view and we gradually reeled them in. By the end of Friday we were only 67 seconds behind, though even that didn't sit well; this was the University of Oregon, the greatest distance-running school on The Planet. We had to do better.

That evening, I organized Part II of the plan. I convinced

three of my Oregon track teammates to run with us the last four miles Saturday. I was a 4:02 miler. It was easy to talk Feig and Matt Centrowitz, a future two-time Olympian, into running. At the time, they were both sub-four milers.

Now it was time for the coup de grâce. I picked up the phone.

"Pre," I said when he answered. "Bence here. We need a relay anchor."

By then, Prefontaine having graduated the year before, he had run a 3:54 mile, one of the best times in the world. "You busy tomorrow?" I told him the plan.

"No, thanks," said Pre, who was still training with the team. "You know we've got a team workout in the morning. Don't wanna run twice."

"I get it," I said, "but it's for a good cause—muscular dystrophy. And you'll finish in front of 41,000 people."

He had no clue what I was talking about; probably thought I'd had a few too many Friday night beers. And, frankly, he didn't seem the least bit interested. But, if only feigning interest, he asked for more details.

"Like, how many schools are in this 'Great Race?'"

"Just two," I said. "Us and Oregon State."

"And who's ahead after Day One?"

"The Beavers—by 67 seconds."

There was a slight pause.

"I'm in," he said.

Oregon was in the midst of a horrible football season—what else was new?—and, with a 2-8 record, was going into the game as a heavy underdog. Pre loved the idea of Oregon winning a running event in Corvallis, in full view of Beavers fans, and in view of the loser Oregon football team, whose players, despite their lack of success, didn't always accord us great respect as athletes. Just like those Nebraska guys.

"By the time you get the baton," I told Pre, "I guarantee you'll have the lead. You just need to extend that lead and flash that great Pre smile once you get to Parker. You'll be running against just a bunch of frat guys. Walk in the park."

I could imagine him already getting that steely gaze in his eyes, the one where he'd glance at the clock coming around the final turn. Success!

After our Saturday morning workout, the four of us drove to our starting point in Corvallis, where the race had left off Friday.

"Holy shit!" I said.

Up ahead of of us, in orange and black, stood four runners from Oregon State's track and field team, including their anchor, Rich Kimball, a freshman who'd run a 4:02 mile in high school.

Uh-oh.

"That guarantee still good on the lead?" Pre asked.

I looked to Feig and Centrowitz, who both offered thumbs up.

We had four miles to go. And making up more than 20 seconds per mile for three of those miles wouldn't be easy. But, hell, I'd gotten us into this mess, I needed to help us get out of it. Feig, Centrowitz, and I hammered away at the lead best we could. But our morning workouts had taken more out of us than we'd expected. We cut 52 seconds off the lead, but when Pre got the batton from Feig he was still 15 seconds behind. And had only a mile to make that up on the talented Kimball.

Mile races are often so competitive that the winner and runner-up might be separated by less than a second; the idea that Pre could make up 15 seconds in only a mile leaned to the foolhardy side. And Pre wasn't pleased when he saw the Beavers still leading. The thought raced through my mind: Would he even agree to run? I saw him peel off his sweats. He shot me a quick "what-about-that-gurarantee?" glance, grabbed the baton, and bolted forward like the cartoon Roadrunner—but not before flipping me off.

I could tell in his eyes that he was going to run hard but a quarter-of-a-minute against a 4:02 miler was a huge handicap. Oh, well. Mark, Matt, and I hopped in a support car and sped off to the stadium to watch the finish. At Parker Stadium, we talked our way onto the field.

The stadium announcer briefly explained The Great Race and directed fans' attention to the north end zone.

"The runners should be entering the stadium at any moment," he said.

Suddenly, down the stadium ramp came a runner who virtually everyone in the stadium recognized. It wasn't some occasional jogger from OSU's Sigma Alpha Epsilon fraternity or a Theta Chi from Oregon. It was the finest US distance runner alive, an Olympian wearing—the crowd all but gasped—green and yellow.

It was Pre.

He was leading an OSU runner—Kimball—by only a stride. It was either man's race.

The football teams, warming up for the second half, had only grudgingly parted to allow the runners down the middle of the field.

"It's Steve Prefontaine from Oregon with a narrow lead on Rich Kimball of Oregon State!" boomed the announcer.

The two sprinted down the middle of the field—10, 20, 30, 40 ....

Pre won by two seconds.

He was ecstatic. The trophy was to have been given to representatives of the winning fraternity, who weren't there, so it was presented to Pre. He milked the moment for all it was worth.

I just stood there with a huge smile on my face. In my short running career, I'd experienced some amazing moments, but nothing as bizarre as this one. You had to love the spirit of Steve Prefontaine.

On the drive back to Eugene—OSU won the game, 35-16—we swapped stories of our respective legs of the run.

"Great day!" said Pre. "Beat the Beavers and did it front of nearly 41,000 Beaver fans and our lazy-ass football team, which doesn't compete with the same gusto we do—the guys they like to make fun of. Hell, maybe next year we'll put on the pads and win the Civil War for them!"

When we got back to Eugene, I asked him for the trophy so I could give to the fraternity.

"Sorry," he said. "Gotta go on the mantle for a little while."

A month later, during the Christmas holiday, I was at Pre's house when I noticed the trophy still there.

"Pre, we really do need to get the trophy to the frat," I said.

"Not yet," he said. "Hell, they didn't win it. We did."

Code for: I did. Oh, well. It made a helluva story.

In the years since, I've remembered that day as one of my favorites. And, given what would happen to Pre the following May, the memory has only become all the more meaningful to me.

Whether it was running in the Olympics or in a two-bit beer relay, Pre only knew one way to race: all out.

Chapter 7
Pre's Last Day

It was late on a Thursday morning—May 29, 1975—when Pre walked into our apartment—without knocking, of course. He was like an honorary roommate. When Pre had recently moved from his trailer in Glenwood to a house in Eugene, we'd put him up for a few weeks during the transition.

"What's up?" he asked.

I wasn't in a particularly talkative mood. Partly because, like everybody else, I was trying to survive Finals Weeks. And partly because my mouth was wired shut because of something that had happened at the the Pac-8 Championships in Pullman twelve days earlier: I'd fallen on my face in a desperate attempt to make a baton exchange in the mile relay. I'd broken my jaw, which was now wired shut. And seventeen stitches decorated the gash on my chin.

"Shhhtudying for tomorrow'shhh math final," came my type-lipped response. I was a senior, wrapping up my last collegiate course. This wasn't how I'd imagined ending my time in the classroom or on the track.

"Conserving energy for tonight," said Feig, relaxing on the living room couch and referring to the Oregon Twilight Meet we'd all be running in.

"Come over to my place," said Pre, less as an invitation than a command. "Centrowitz is on his way; it will be the four of us. Bencie, bring your math book."

We agreed, following him in Mark's car through the quiet Eugene neighborhoods to his new digs. As you might expect, the place wasn't exactly decorated from the pages of *Home Beautiful*; in fact, about the only noteworthy item was The Great Race trophy on his fireplace mantel. Over the years, Pre had won trophies galore; he was the finest distance runner in America. But what he put on his mantel was that crazy frat-race cup.

As we gathered at his coffee table on that sunny May day, I didn't study; that was just Pre's ploy to get us over to his house. Instead, we played Spades. Pre was always hyper before a race and needed the distraction of playing cards to settle him.

"Open your mouth," Pre said to me, then winced at the sight of the wires holding my jaw together. "You're gonna run with that?"

"No choish," I said. "I don't have an en-shee-a-a qualifying time; thish ish my lasht chance."

The accident had happened in the Pac-8-Championships-from-Hell less than two weeks earlier. Nobody other than Washington State liked competing in Pullman. "Why go all the way up there to run on a cement-hard track in who-knows-what kind of weather in front of a handful of fans?" moaned UCLA Coach Jim Bush to our student paper, the *Oregon Daily Emerald*, a few days before the event.

For Oregon, everything that could go wrong did—from decathlete Craig Brigham snapping a pole in the pole vault—fortunately, he wasn't hurt—to seasoned vets, myself included, just not pulling through. I'd finished only fourth in the 880 (1:50.9) and, sitting on a bench, hung my head in frustration, the insult-to-injury being that a photographer for the *The Emerald*, captured the moment and, in Monday's paper, made me famous for my failure. Finally, in a desperate attempt to help us finish third instead of fourth, Dellinger had thrown me into the last event, the mile relay.

I ran hard on the third leg, tying up as I approached the handoff to an anxious Dave Hagmeier, who took off early, forcing me to dive in a failed attempt to pass the baton. I hit chin-first on that rock-hard track in what felt like a left hook from Muhammad Ali. I laid there until trainers helped me up. While our bus waited, I was stitched up in the WSU training room.

On the flight home from Spokane, my left jaw hurt like hell. Feig's dad, who was traveling with the team, bought two drinks for me on the flight, which was thoughtful and, to some degree, helpful. Still, I was a mess.

Back in Eugene, X-rays showed my jaw was broken. My mouth, doctors decided, needed to be wired shut. I checked into Sacred Heart Hospital, was put under general anesthesia, and awoke hours later with Mary in my hospital room.

"How did it go?" I asked groggily.

"Look in the mirror."

I wished I hadn't. My mouth and cheeks were covered in freshly dried blood, apparently from whatever it took to do the wiring. Most of it washed off, leaving me with a gleaming metallic smile. Meanwhile, my face, jaw, and teeth ached as if I'd run full-speed into a brick wall.

"Did the doctor say anything?" I asked.

"He said it went well and you need to put together a liquid meal plan. The blender is going to be your new best friend."

Now, a week had passed since that hospital visit. Between missing training and missing calories, I was going into the Twilight Meet nowhere near top shape. But Thursday's meet was my last hope to hit the 1:49.7 standard for the NCAA. And I was a senior; fail to qualify and my college career was over.

Pre was impressed with my determination. "Crazy, man."

He turned to Matt. "You're running the half as well?"

"Yeah. I've been working on my speed; thought I should run a shorter race. I want to see what I can do; it'll help me in the mile."

Mark was entered in the mile. "You already qualified," Pre said to him. "Shouldn't you rest this week for the NCAAs? Take it easy? Why are you racing?"

"Because I ran like shit in the Pac-8s—seventh in 4:13. I need a confidence boost."

Pre seemed particularly hyper as the subject turned to— what else?—track and field. Never one to shy away from a fight, he had famously butted heads with the AAU for years over how shabbily they treated US athletes. Adding to that pressure was his decision to bring Finnish athletes to Oregon for a series of meets, including that night's Twilight Meet. But would anyone show up?

After years of going to Europe and seeing how small towns would put on grand track and field meets, Pre thought: why not do that here? So, he'd invited a Finnish contingent to Oregon for a series of meets, this being the finale. From the get-go, it was obvious that he was in over his head; he wouldn't have pulled it off without the help of Nike running promo man Geoff Hollister, who could look the idealistic Prefontiane in the eye and ask the tough questions. "So how you going to get the poles of the Finnish pole vaulters from the airport to Hayward Field—in your MG?" Well, of course, Pre had never thought of that; his speciality was dreaming, not the nuts-and-bolts strategy of actually pulling off the dream.

Admittedly, there was a bit of "Trojan Horse" to his plan. Yes, the Finns had treated him great when he was over there; he loved the whole idea of European and American athletes "making the world smaller" by competing against each other and throwing back some beers afterward. But beyond such things, he wanted another shot at Lasse Viren, who'd won gold in the 1972 Olympic 5000-meter in which Pre had faded to fourth—the rematch to be on the Hayward Field track where he'd never lost a race in anything over a mile. But Pre's hope for revenge ended about ten days earlier when he received a telegram saying Viren would have to scratch due to injury. Pre was bummed.

"How about you, Pre?" I asked. "How you doing?"

"The past month's been hard, harder than I expected. At least the AAU backed off, those assholes. They do nothing for the athletes and then when we do something for ourselves, for our sport—invite the Finns to Oregon—they threaten to sanction us. How about a little help, some encouragement?"

"Too bad about Viren," I said.

"He probably read that I broke the American 2000-meter record in Coos Bay," he said, more serious than not. "That probably scared him."

"You OK financially?" Mark asked, knowing Pre was sinking some of his own money into all this and too busy to work.

"Who knows? I was counting on a good gate receipt tonight to cover expenses. Without Viren here, attendance might be weak."

With great bravado, Pre had vowed to break his American 5000-meter record at the meet. But after Viren scratched, he'd had to talk Frank Shorter, the 1972 Olympic marathon champion, into running against him in the 5k to help him meet that goal.

"I hope the stands will be at least half full," he said.

As the conversation continued, Pre questioned how prepared he was, mentally and physically, to run well. I ignored him. He was forever complaining about not being in decent shape—though not publicly—and was forever breaking records anyway.

We played a few more games, then needed to get ready for the meet.

He headed into his bedroom to change into his uniform: a black Norditalia singlet, which I assumed he'd gotten while competing in Italy; a Colorado tee shirt, a gift, I believe, from Shorter, who'd trained in Colorado for two years prior to the 1972 Olympics; white shorts, and USA sweats.

For some reason, when Pre came out, he suddenly looked at the frat trophy on the mantel.

"Hey, let's take a picture," Pre said.

He picked up his camera, the trophy, and ran next door to get his neighbor to take our picture in the front yard. Who does that? And just as we were all mentally transitioning to this big meet in a few hours. But Pre had this charisma, this unspoken ability to control situations—not in a bad way, but definitely in his own way. We laughed, remembering the relay race that Pre had anchored in front of the partisan Beaver football fans in Corvallis.

We posed for a photo and Pre handed the trophy to me.

"Bencie, it's time," he said—six months since he'd nabbed it after the race. "Give it to the fraternity. I've had my run with it."

I mentally rolled my eyes. Why now? Why, of all times, does he give up the trophy just as we're leaving for a big meet? Weird.

We drove to our apartment, the rest of us changed, and we jogged the half mile to Hayward Field, sharing Pre's anxiety about the crowd size. What we found thrilled us. The stadium was filling fast. "Sweet!" Pre said. His people had shown up after all.

The shadows at Hayward were starting to lengthen. Former Duck runner Kenny Moore, accompanied by a photographer, was covering the meet for *Sports Illustrated*. I nodded a hello and started warming up for the 880, which was to be run at 7:20 p.m., about an hour before sunset.

Soon I heard the loudspeaker announcement that sent my gut into edgy anticipation.

"Last call, 880 yards! Last call, 880!"

I didn't have my usual confidence before a race, the feeling that I could run whatever I was capable of. When I had a bad race it was usually because of tactics: getting boxed in or running my first lap either too fast or too slow. But in the past four years I had become experienced, learning from my mistakes. Now, as the race neared, my fear wasn't strategy, but something deeper.

I was now living the high-anxiety dream of showing up to class, discovering it was a final exam, and realizing I hadn't studied. Only this wasn't a dream; I couldn't wake up. This was real. I felt unprepared because my nutrition intake and training hadn't been what they should have been for the past 12 days. But I couldn't sit out this race either; there would be no "next race." It was do-or-die. I started thinking how I could gracefully drop out if I found myself struggling.

As I sat in the infield pen, Pre leaned over and gave my shoulder a tug of encouragement. The *SI* photographer snapped several pictures of the two of us. (See Page 98 and the back cover.)

"I don't think I could do what you're doing," said Pre, looking at my wired-shut mouth, "so why not make it worthwhile?"

I nodded, stayed silent, and Prefontaine withdrew to watch and prepare for his race.

I needed to run 1:49.8 to qualify for the NCAA Championships. It had been an amazing—and, here and there, frustrating—four years. And my only chance to "stay out and play a little longer" was to qualify for the NCAA meet.

We were introduced and jogged over to the starting line in our respective lanes. Centrowitz was in an outer lane, Ebba and I in the first two lanes. We wished each other luck. This was probably my tenth race against Hailu over the years, indoors and outdoors; I think I beat him in all but one, an Oregon-vs.-Oregon-State dual meet at Hayward Field when he beat Feig in the mile and came back to beat me in the half. I considered Hailu a friend and knew that he would do whatever he could to help me qualify.

"One-forty-nine-eight?" Hailu asked.

I nodded yes.

"Let me lead," he said. He would be my rabbit, my pacemaker.

A second nod.

"To your marks!" yelled longtime starter Ray Hendrickson, the principal at North Eugene High.

Utter silence.

"Sehhhhhhhhhhhhhhhhhhhht."

I exhaled. The crowd hushed. At the crack of the starter's pistol, I bolted forward. I ran steady and confident for the first lap and a half. With 220 yards left, I glanced at the clock. Hailu set a good pace. Though my arms felt heavy, I had a chance.

"Relax!" Pre yelled at me from the infield. He knew that when I got tired, my arms tended to tighten up, and my legs followed suit. "Drop your arms!"

I did. Ebba began pulling away. I tried to stay with him, knowing that he could pull me to 1:49.8 or better. But though I tried to find that next gear, it wasn't there, lost in nearly two weeks of meager workouts. I lumbered home, my legs feeling as if caked with ice.

"Hailu Ebba of Oregon State wins in 1:49.7!" said the announcer.

Such precision, almost exactly what I needed. He'd done his part; I just hadn't done mine. Couldn't do mine.

My heart sank; clearly I hadn't made it. I finished second in 1:50.8, a second slower than what I needed. If I could have stayed with Ebba, I would have qualified. My college career was over. I bent over after the finish, hands on hips, staring blankly at the ground. It had been my last race as a Duck.

"Hey, Bence," said another runner, "you set a world record—for guys running with their mouths wired shut."

I forced a smile, nodding at him for softening a moment that, deep down hurt as if I'd been stabbed with a rusty knife.

Ten minutes later, Feig just missed another sub-four, running 4:00.4, finishing second to Gary Barger (3:58.8), who became the sixteenth Oregon runner to break the magical four-minute barrier. Though he hadn't cracked four, Feig had found the confidence booster he needed.

Pre's race was the final event, just before 8 p.m. By then the crowd had swelled to 8,000 fans. One by one, the entrants in the 5000 meters were introduced: Dave Taylor (UO), Rune Holmen (Finland), Jon Anderson (OTC), Randy Brown (OSU), Tom McChesney (UO), Bob Smith (UO), Rod Cooper (Lane Community College), Frank Shorter (Florida Track Club), and then, as the announcer spoke it, simply "Pre."

The Hayward crowd erupted in delight.

The gun went off. Pre and Shorter ran together, paced by "rabbits" Geis and Terry Williams, 4:17 for the first mile, a 64-second pace that, if maintained, would break Pre's 13:21.9 American record. They slowed to a 66-second pace for the second mile, and then Shorter slowed to a 68-second pace for the third.

With 2½ laps to go, Pre accelerated. Shorter fell back. Pre won in 13:23.8, missing his personal best by 2 seconds. The Hayward Field fans were on their feet, appreciative of the effort, even if disappointed he'd missed the American record he had promised.

Pre took a couple victory laps, then was swarmed by adoring fans, among them young boys waving their programs that he gladly autographed. I just stood there, marveling at his warm, authentic relationship with his people, feeling honored to call him a friend.

At what seemed like the right moment, Pre signaled that he had to leave. He waved goodbye to his fans—for the last time, it turned out. The four of us jogged back to the apartment, showered, and readied to head our different directions for the evening.

"Bencie," Pre said. "I'm giving you tomorrow off but Saturday you're starting your post-collegiate training. And I'm your coach."

I just shook my head. I'd never given any serious thought to my future running plans, if any, after college. But when Pre invited you into something—whether it was a party or a game of Spades or coaching you—it was hard to turn him down. It was as if he was this wild, rushing river—the McKenzie below Bowerman's perch—and those of us around him—fans, friends, teammates—counted it a privilege to simply ride the rapids.

Pre rushed off; the guy was always in a hurry. Apparently, he was headed for a private party to honor the Finnish guests. Meanwhile, Mark and I went to the team awards banquet at the Black Angus Restaurant on Franklin. We got back late. I had more studying to do before my Friday final, but, like the homestretch against Ebba, I had nothing left to give. I had to sleep; studying would have to wait until morning. I hit the pillow, the disappointment of not having made the NCAAs lost in my desire to crash.

A ringing phone jarred me awake the next morning at 6 o'clock. The call was from a former teammate who'd said something that, in the haze of my just having been awakened, I could barely comprehend.

"Bencie," he said, "I was driving to work and heard that Pre died. Is it true?"

What? Naw. I'd just seen him. Couldn't be true.

"I don't think so," I said "Just saw him last night. We had a meet. I'll check."

I called KUGN, the radio station that broadcast Duck sports, and told them about the rumor I'd heard.

"It's not a rumor," the receptionist said. "Pre died early this morning in a single-car accident."

I froze in disbelief.

I walked into Mark's room and stood at the foot of his bed as he sat up. There was an awkward silence as I saw Mark's expression turn from confusion to concern.

I gulped. "Pre's dead." It was all I could say, it was all I knew, and I left the room.

I walked to the Erb Memorial Union cafeteria on campus to study, be around people, try to burrow away far from the truth—as if I by ignoring it, the tragedy might not be true. It was a beautiful day, perfect temperature, bright blue sky, white billowy clouds. Just the opposite of my internal gloom.

I sat at a cafeteria table half-studying, everything around me seeming too normal, too routine. Did anybody understand what just happened? Did anyone care?

Chicago's song "Wishing You Were Here" was playings in the background. I listened to the words and the emotion of the music, and finally it hit me.

Pre's gone.

Suddenly, I couldn't stop the tears.

By the time I returned to the apartment, Mark had already been interviewed by *The Register-Guard*. We talked. In late afternoon, I went out to find a copy of Friday's newspaper. "Pre's death the end of an era" shouted the headline. "Nation's top distance runner killed in single-car accident."

I imagined someone yelling "Stop the presses!" as reporters scrambled to put together the breaking stories. I scanned the front-page story, handed the "A" section to Mark, and turned to the sports section. One headline grabbed my attention: "His Friends remember Prefontaine."

"It says you are the Oregon runner probably closest to Pre," I said to Mark. "You're quoted, 'It was hard to get to know him. He was an idol of mine even though I was running with him, and I was at his place with some guys playing cards yesterday before the meet.'"

Mark studied the map of the accident on the front-page.

"It happened on Skyline," he said.

"Where's that?"

Mark had grown up in Eugene. "It dead-ends at Birch Street, the road we run up to get to Hendricks Park."

I never really paid attention to the streets signs. "I don't think I've ever been on Skyline."

"There's a big curve about 150 feet from the intersection, where the accident happened. We can run up there tomorrow."

We kept reading, trying to make sense of the three hours after we last saw him.

Mark read aloud. "It says, 'Pre and his girlfriend, Nancy Alleman, appeared at the Black Angus Restaurant where the Oregon track team was having its awards dinner. He stayed only 10 minutes and then told Dellinger he was going to the farewell party for the Finnish athletes at Geoff Hollister's house.'"

"I didn't see him," I said.

"Really? I did. He stopped briefly to talk to Dellinger; they probably didn't talk after his race. Pre must have picked up Nancy on his way to Geoff's house, stopped at the Paddock for a couple of beers."

"Ha! That sounds like him," I said. "They probably scarfed a Bea's burger as well."

Mark resumed reading aloud. "It was a well-attended party at Hollister's house with Pre's parents, his high school coach Walt McClure, Jaakko Tuominen with the Finns, Kenny Moore and his wife, and other friends and acquaintances."

"Here's a quote from Shorter: 'Anytime you party with New Zealanders or Finns there is drinking. We left about 12:15, got into the MG and drove down to the UO ticket office where Nancy left her car, and dropped her off. I wasn't afraid to ride with Pre, he drove me to Kenny's house. We had a short conversation before I got out of the car, agreed to a time to run on Saturday, and Pre headed down the hill.'"

Said the paper:

> Prefontaine was apparently unable to make the turn. The car went over the curb, striking a solid natural rock embankment. The car flipped over and came to rest upside down, pinning Prefontaine's chest between the driver's door and the pavement. There was no indication of excessive speed. There were about 40 feet of skid marks from the center line to the curb.
>
> Bill Alvarado, who lived nearby, said he heard the screech of tires and a thunk, left his home, saw a second light-colored MGB speeding up Skyline Boulevard away from Pre's overturned car.
>
> The driver of the second MGB told officers that he came across the overturned car, apparently moments after the crash and decided to drive to his nearby home to get help from his father, who is a doctor.
>
> "I hate to say it," Alvarado said, "but I couldn't do anything. I couldn't lift the car; my back still aches from trying. I had no idea who it was under the car. I knew Pre's car, but I was hoping it wasn't him."

That was enough for this day, May 30, 1975. Mark and I stopped reading. I felt empty. I had taken my last exam, barely able to concentrate. My undergraduate studies were completed. I had finished my last race as an Oregon Duck, not the race I hoped for. A friend and teammate had just died.

I thought back to what Bowerman had said at our incoming freshman meeting. "Look around you. Chances are that only three or four of you will still be on the track team your senior year."

He was right: Feig, Tinker Hatfield, and I were all that was left from that freshman class.

Bowerman had also said, "You are here first for an education, and there is no reason you can't all graduate." I was about to do so. But now what?

What about my finding purpose through running, which had helped me find meaning in life so far? That seemed impossible now. My career was over. My friend was dead. My future was as hazy as February fog hanging over the Willamette.

I couldn't see any future. All I could see was a kid staring back in a mirror—a kid whose face seemed stained with either fear or uncertainty.

Maybe both.

Only hours before Pre would die, he looked at me and my broken jaw. "I don't think I could do what you're doing," he said, "so why not make it worthwhile?"

PART II

TRANSITION

Change will not come if we wait for some other person or some other time. We are the ones we've been waiting for. We are the change that we seek.

—**Barack Obama**

Chapter 8
Goodbye

A light blue hearse carrying Pre's body drove around the track at Marshfield High's Pirate Stadium, a jarring juxtaposition. This was among the places where Pre was most alive; now, the hearse spoke only of death. The crowd of 2,500 was in the grandstands, locals and visitors alike watching Pre's last lap on the same track where it all had started eight years earlier.

It was here three weeks earlier where Mark and I had run when the Finns were in Oregon. Prefontaine had broken the American record for 2000 meters in front of the same people who were now here to mourn his death.

I was deep in thought, as I had been over the previous days since Pre died. Like many others, I looked up to Pre, I was inspired by him, and we were friends. But watching the pallbearers carry his casket, I knew this: I didn't want to die young. And I kept wondering about this: Why, of all days, had he chosen his last to finally let go of that crazy fraternity's trophy?

Pre was intense every day, almost as if he knew he was living on borrowed time. When he stayed with Mark and me, sleeping on the couch, I barely saw him. He usually came home after midnight and was gone before I woke up, getting in his morning run before having a quick breakfast. I could never match his daily pace, accomplishing all that he did while never missing a workout nor race.

His secret was more than just the immense talent that he was born with—it was his persistence, consistency, and his ability to avoid serious sickness or injury.

The part of Pre that I most wanted to emulate was his passion and determination to speak up for important causes such as his fight against the AAU, which was a battle for the rights of amateur athletes like me. He was outspoken, a lightning rod for criticism, a catalyst for change. I was determined to find opportunities in the future to bravely speak up like Pre, to make a difference.

As the ceremony at Marshfield High began, two of Pre's former coaches, high school coach Walt McClure and Bowerman, delivered eulogies. A gift from the Finnish athletes was presented to the Prefontaine family. Then the family went to the Coos Bay Cemetery for the burial; meanwhile, we drove back to Eugene.

Later that day, Mark, Mary, and I walked from the apartment to Hayward Field and watched the stands fill to about 3,500 for yet another service. If Coos Bay was Pre's home, Eugene was his second home, a city that had embraced the guy as soon as he'd hit town in fall 1969.

Our attention was directed to the scoreboard at the south end of Hayward Field as the clocked started to methodically tick towards 12:36, a time representing a world record for three miles, a time that Pre had once said would "satisfy" him.

There were a few remarks from Moore, Shorter, and

Bowerman. I couldn't tell you what they said; I wasn't really listening. My mind was cluttered with too many memories, my soul racked with too much sadness, my ears hearing nothing but the stillness of a life—a legend—now gone.

The tribute wasn't about Pre's accomplishments, not about what he did—we already knew that—but about how he lived. I vowed to hold myself to Pre's higher standard, something bigger than winning, to pursue a life focused on the people around me and to build authentic relationships. Maybe, I wondered, I had found my deeper purpose—a bit of focus amid my blurry view of the future.

I looked at the other people in the stadium around me. In better days, these same people had been fans watching a track meet, rising out of their seats to cheer wildly in support of Pre. Today, I saw only tears. Heard only sniffles. Felt only emptiness.

The clock stopped at 12:36.2. There was warm applause, followed by more silence. A handful started to leave and, gradually, others left as they were ready. Soon Hayward Field was once again empty.

For more than a week, the sports page of *The Register-Guard* ran numerous articles about Pre, accompanied by an outpouring of letters, tributes, pictures, and poems from around the world.

That helped me.

I loved *Guard* sports columnist Blaine Newnham's reflections.

> Pre didn't have much use for sports writers. Most sports writers didn't have much use for Pre. He was arrogant, he was impatient, he could be rude, and he eschewed small talk.
>
> When I first met him a mere four years ago, at the 1971 USA-Russian track meet in Berkeley, I mentioned his race against the Russians. I asked about his strategy,

his pace. His eyes twinkled. He leaned back against the edge of the balcony and started talking.

"I thought you weren't going to talk to sports writers anymore."

Pre replied that I hadn't asked any stupid questions yet.

That article reminded me of a heated moment at Pre's house a couple of months earlier. He had a *Track & Field News* article posted in his kitchen—and someone had asked him about it, which set him off.

"This is yet another example of a sportswriter twisting my words. Francie Larrieu has been killing it in the indoor mile. I like Francie, we get along well. She broke her own world mile indoor record in San Diego and a reporter called to talk about it. We talked about how well Francie has been running, and women running in general. I'm not against women athletes; in fact, I'm quite the opposite. Then he asked me if women would ever catch up to the men and run comparable times. You can read my one sentence that made it into the article. I don't get it, I'm speaking up for US athletes, both men and women, but reporters already have their story in their heads and are just looking for a quote to spice it up. I end up looking like a jerk."

I read the article for Pre's quote.

It read, "I admire her tremendously, and I wish I could match her dedication. But the fact is, her 4:29 was a world record for women and I can run six 4:29s in a row."

Vintage Pre, speaking truth without thinking how he might sound out of context. He never was one to hold back.

Mark finished packing and was ready to join the team to fly to Provo for the 1975 NCAA Track and Field Championships. Since I didn't qualify, I was staying home. Mark showed me the black armbands that he would give to the other Oregon athletes to wear in memory of Pre.

"Take one," Mark said, handing me an armband. "By the

way, did you know that you're entered in the Prefontaine Classic? Wear it Saturday."

I was still dwelling on all my losses: a chance to run in a fourth and final NCAA, and Pre. And if not a loss of innocence, a loss of security or idealism or comfort—the idea that we all could run and laugh and be crazy-assed college kids the rest of our lives.

Pre's death chilled me. I took the armband.

The Oregon Track Club, with Bowerman's blessing, voted to rename Saturday's Hayward Restoration Meet, whose proceeds would go to the building of the new West Grandstands, the Steve Prefontaine Classic. Meet director Bob Newland insisted it was strictly a low-budget OTC meet, yet he lined up four athletes who ranked No. 1 in the world, and three athletes who ranked No. 2.

With the meet now carrying Pre' name, it was poised to compete with the best meets in the country, maybe in the world. But only about 8,000 fans showed up. Ironically, without Pre as the headliner, attendance lagged compared to previous years.

Don Quarrie and Steve Williams both ran faster than the existing 220 world record, another world record for Hayward Field. In my race, the 880, Rick Wohlhuter ran a sizzling 1:45.4, only about a second short of his world half-mile world record set at Hayward the previous year, followed by Hailu Ebba, and Ken Sparks. With my jaw still wired shut, I was fourth; my friend Hailu had beaten me for the second time in two weeks.

Tom Jordan, a well-known meet organizer from Eugene, began interviewing people for a book he was going to write about Pre and asked for stories from his teammates. I wrote what stood out to me, which Jordan included in the book: Pre's competitiveness, impatience, the longer runs I shared with him, his most impressive workouts, and my favorite Prefontaine race—weirdly, a two-mile event in an obscure meet in Corvallis.

No, not the frat relay; more obscure than even that.

It was an iconic moment for Pre and Geis, a moment you can only appreciate when fully understanding their rivalry. A moment that reminded me that the two were more alike than they were different. I told Jordan about how misunderstood their rivalry was to track fans. When Geis first moved from Rice to Oregon, there was no problem. Paul was a good runner, but not a threat to Pre. But as Geis improved, the press called him Pre's "heir-apparent," putting pressure on Geis, and putting Pre on the defensive. They started to race each other in practice, which Dellinger discouraged. I blamed the press for creating the unnecessary tension. There was no replacing Pre; he was simply graduating from college and had a future. But the press fanned the flames of the Pre-Geis rivalry, knowing it would make great headlines.

At any rate, Dellinger wanted to use a low-key two-mile race at Oregon State as a time trial for the two runners. "Don't go all out," he told them. "Just shoot for 8:35—and cross the finish line together. Got that? Together."

It was like asking the US and the Soviet Union to share a group hug. But as the race unfurled, it looked to me as if they were obliging Dellinger. When they came down home stretch, they not only remained running in unison, but just before the finish line, Geis suddenly did something that made my eyes bulge: he reached out to grab Pre's hand, and the two finished hand-in-hand, in 8:35.8, staring at each other as they crossed the finish line. I didn't know whether to laugh or wince. What had just happened?

"Nice show of teamwork," I said to Geis after the race.

"Hell, that wasn't teamwork," he said. "That was pride. Neither of us trusted the other to not lunge at the last second."

Chapter 9
Life Beyond Track

In late summer 1975 Mark, Mary, and I found an apartment on Eugene's Country Club Road. Mark worked at the store of that upstart shoe company, Nike, called The Athletic Department, in downtown Eugene. Meanwhile, Mary was wrapping up her senior year at UO and I was focusing on getting my teaching certificate.

I did my student teaching at North Eugene High, a track-friendly school. Kenny Moore had graduated from NEHS, Olympian Mike Manley was a teacher and cross-country coach there, and Newland—the highly respected meet organizer—was vice principal.

I was assigned to a math teacher who was a great mentor. After I asked Manley if I could be his assistant cross-country coach, he welcomed me aboard. He wrote the workouts and I served as part coach and part teammate, often running the workouts with the guys.

I gave equal time and encouragement to everyone on the team and found that the time I spent with the slower runners was the most valuable. Though cross-country teams field seven runners, only the top five scored points. I knew that a team championship usually came down to the No. 4 and 5 runners. So, on the longer training runs I often dropped to the back of the pack, keeping those guys moving and motivated.

We placed third in the Midwest League meet, qualifying for the Class AAA State Championships. South Eugene was the overwhelming favorite to win state, which they did with 32 points. However, North Eugene, led by Mike Friton and Bill Gilmore, narrowly edged Cottage Grove for second in state— and our 4-5 guys had made the difference. I was a proud coach; it was a rewarding moment!

In fall 1975, Mary's parents, Joe and MD, came to Eugene from Portland for a football game. We met them for a drink before the game in their New Oregon Hotel room. Joe invited us to dinner after the game at his favorite Eugene restaurant, Louie's Village, on Franklin Boulevard, across from the UO.

It was time to make the engagement of Mary and me official. I knew Joe was Italian, which intimidated me, probably because of the 1972 *Godfather* movie. I had the irrational thought that he was a member of the mob and might bump me off if he didn't like the idea of me marrying his daughter. I didn't know whether to call him Joe or Mr. Jacko; he never suggested how I should address him, so I avoided calling him by name.

At just the right moment in the conversation, when I had Joe's attention and wouldn't have to say his name, I mustered the courage to speak.

"Uh, I'd like to ask your permission to marry your daughter."

"Which daughter?" he said, momentarily derailing me. Then he laughed. "Of course, Steve. You have our permission, our blessing. Do you have a date?"

A date? Hell, not a clue.

Mary saved me. "This summer. We'll find a date that works for everyone."

My heart was racing. MD jumped into the conversation. I relaxed, and it sunk in. I was engaged!

"What are your plans?" Joe asked.

"Get my teaching certificate after the new year. I'll substitute-teach while Mary finishes her degree. Then the wedding this summer, and I'll look for a full-time teaching-and-coaching job, hopefully in Europe where I graduated high school."

MD and Joe knew that I'd grown up in a military family; heck, they met while serving in the Army in England during World War II, Joe part of a medical unit and MD a nurse. They married before moving back to the States. Joe served in a MASH unit during the Korean War; they understood overseas assignments.

"How about your running career?" Joe asked.

"I'll keep training through the spring and run a few races. Ideally, I'll run in the Olympic Trials again, but it will be difficult to get in the proper training to qualify with all that's happening."

"Whatever happens with your running," Joe said, "you should be proud at what you've accomplished."

I appreciated that. And I think Joe appreciated that I had a plan involving his daughter.

In January 1976, I was eligible to substitute teach. I was on call, getting up every morning to prepare to go to work because I would often get short notice for an assignment.

To supplement my income, I worked at Murphy & Me, a hippie off-campus tavern. The place had live music, which didn't really interest me except for a regular band called Wheatfield. One evening I invited Mary to hear them, eager to have her hear my favorite song done by the band.

"That's not a Wheatfield song," Mary explained after hearing it, "it's a Beatles song. Didn't you follow the Beatles in the 1960s? That song is called 'I've Just Seen a Face' and was in the movie *Help!*"

"I think I missed a lot growing up at Edwards Air Force Base."

A few weeks later at the tavern, I had an encounter with a drunk, belligerent customer.

"You're home early," Mary observed when I arrived.

"I got stabbed in the back," I said. "Literally."

"What? Turn around. Take off your shirt."

"Stabbed?" she laughed. "That's a scratch."

OK, maybe I'd overstated the results of my altercation with a customer. But that was the end of Murphy & Me. I resigned.

Mark and Mary worked at the Paddock Tavern, which was more a sports bar where students, athletes, and fans congregated. I belonged there. The Paddock-over-Murphy-&-Me lesson was this: in looking for a future job, I needed to understand the culture of an organization and find the right fit—for me. And, preferably, a place without back-stabbing.

My best chance of getting a job in Europe was to take a gamble by going there and seeing if I could get hired somewhere. The plan was to save enough money, buy a round-trip ticket to Germany, leave right after the wedding, stay for three weeks, and if I couldn't get a job in Europe, return to Oregon to find a job.

The approach seemed logical to me. My life had been a series of moves around the world and finding my way in life once I arrived, not turning back. This time I had a safety net; if it didn't work out, I had a home to return to.

Mary and MD settled on a date for the wedding, August 7, 1976, at Saint Rita's Catholic Church in Northeast Portland. The reception was to be in the Jacko's back yard.

"Let me get this straight," I said to Mary and her father. "When MD came home from the hospital after giving birth to Mary, this was the same house you brought her to?"

"That's right, Steve," said Joe. That was a hard thing to grasp for a kid who'd bounced from place to place more than the Harlem Globetrotters. When my mother came home with me, our family was living in Tennessee, though I remembered nothing about the house whatsoever.

I didn't have much to do nor say about the wedding. "Just do what you're told," said Mary. "Wear what you're given, show up to the church on time, and don't be drunk or hung over."

I complied. With the exception of Mary's brother, Mark, the groomsmen were mostly friends on the track team. I invited OSU's Hailu Ebba, who made the three-hour round-trip drive from Corvallis to attend as a welcomed friend. With a few exceptions, I had a good relationship with most of the people I raced against; there was a culture of honor and respect among us.

The wedding and reception were great. The next day, Joe and MD took us to the airport, and we left for the three weeks in Germany. A new adventure had begun. Or so we thought. I was hoping USDESEA would have a last-minute need for a teacher and coach somewhere in Europe; I was there and willing to move anywhere. But that wasn't the case; no job offer emerged. Rather than waiting for an opportunity, I talked Mary into getting a two-week Eurail pass so we could travel.

"Our European honeymoon!" I wanted to believe.

"I wouldn't call traveling around Europe on a shoestring budget a honeymoon," she said. "You still owe me a proper honeymoon." I agreed.

It was September 1976; the school year in Oregon had just started. I had several leads for teaching jobs with one that looked promising. There was a need in Beaverton at Five Oaks Middle School for a teacher to cover two general math classes (I was a math major), an algebra/computer science class (I took college classes in computer programming), a first-year Spanish class (I had lived in Spain), and a first-period conditioning class (I had run at UO). The job was a perfect match for me and I was hired on a one-year contract.

Mary found a job with US Bank. Meanwhile, Feig had been promoted to be in charge of the handful of Nike retail stores in Oregon, and needed to move to the Portland area. He asked if he could rent the second bedroom in our Beaverton apartment. Hey, the three of us had lived together so long it almost seemed weird without him. We loved Mark and he would help pay the rent. We were a trio again.

During spring break 1977, Mary and I went to Mountain Home Air Force Base in Idaho to visit with my parents at their latest stop in their hop-scotching around the world. Mary and my parents had never spent any quality time together, so this allowed us a few days for just the four of us.

My father, Steve Jr., had a small boat with an outboard motor, and he loved fishing. He took Mary and me to his favorite Idaho fishing spot in the early morning. There is a difference between fishing and catching; my father loved the former. He didn't need to be hauling in tons of fish to enjoy himself.

My mother had packed us a lunch and we found a picnic table on the shore where we ate. We were close as father-son, but I don't think I'd had an authentic, real conversation with the man since high school. After World War II, he had had a four-year assignment in Japan in an advisory role. He served in the Korean War in the early '50s. I was born eight months and three weeks after he returned to the States; as my mother said, the second thing he did was put down his duffle bag. While I was in college, Dad, in his early 40s, served in the Vietnam War at Thailand's Nakhon Phanom Air Force Base.

"Dad," I asked, "what was it like—being in Nam?"

While some of the older guys in my Baby Boom generation had gone to Vietnam, most had found a way—with college deferments—to avoid it. None of my friends had gone to

Vietnam.

"It was an assignment that I volunteered for," he said. "I received combat pay which I saved, and they took good care of me. I lost weight, probably too much; I didn't eat like I should have. Overall, it was boring with the exception of the four o'clock afternoon mortars lobbed in to remind us that the Vietcong were nearby. I avoided being in the wrong place at the wrong time."

He asked about my future plans; I asked about his.

"I'm 46 years old. I would like to make it to 30 years with the Air Force, earn my final stripe to maximize retirement pay, and be retired by age 50. Then I want to move to Ohio with your mom, build a house with a small pond, and stock it with so many fish that you could walk across the water on their backs. If you want to find me, you'll know where to look."

Back at the base, my mother and I found time to talk alone—less of a rarity than talking to my father.

"I've lived the life of a gypsy, and that of a military wife," she said. "As a child I moved from West Virginia, to southern Ohio, to Cleveland as a secretary. I was a stewardess, and met your dad. Then we traveled the world with the military, never putting down any roots, or developing any long-term relationships.

"Your dad has a dream to settle down in Ohio and fish. I'm OK with the part about Ohio, because there are colleges within a short drive wherever we'd live. I can't help him in building a house, I can't hit a nail on its head. I'd like to study, get a college degree—and perhaps a degree beyond that. I think your dad is threatened that I will become more educated than him."

Back in Beaverton, Mark was prodding me again, as he did when he introduced Mary as my girlfriend.

"Steve," he said, "you need to work part-time at the Nike Beaverton store. I can arrange it."

I was taking a Portland State class towards a master's degree in education, but merely going through the motions. I agreed, I needed to get out of the apartment more. I took the job. The store job energized me; it was much better than teaching. I was interacting with people who cared about running and I was learning what consumers wanted in product, especially the shoes that I cared about.

Unlike my job at Murphy & Me, or as a teacher, Nike had an inviting culture that suited me. And most importantly, there might be an opportunity to move overseas.

"Bencie," Mark pressed, "you should submit your resume for a full-time job at Nike."

I was still in the interviewing process for a teaching job but I gave my resume to Mark to submit to Nike on my behalf. The company scheduled an interview with me at the Beaverton Headquarters on Tuesday July 12, 1977.

The evening before my interview, my mother called; I had no idea why. This wasn't like her.   Mark and Mary were gone; I was home alone in the apartment.

"Stephen, are you sitting down?"

"No, Mom, it's OK. What's up?"

"Your father died."

Chapter 10
Beginning with Nike

I dropped to my knees on the floor, as if Mom's words pressed "Pause" on my brain. I realized that she was still talking to me but I didn't understand a word she was saying. She must have sensed what I was going through.

"Stephen, you probably need a moment. I'll call you back in ten minutes."

This wasn't happening, right? It had been a short two years since Pre died; now my father?

I made a quick call to Mary, who was with her sisters. I couldn't explain what happened, because I didn't know yet. Mary drove home immediately. I composed myself and Mom called back.

"How are you doing?" I asked Mom.

"Can you come here for a of couple days?" she asked. "I need help."

Come to Idaho? What the hell was she talking about? My dad was only 46 years old. I'd just spent a day fishing with him. He couldn't have died.

"Uh, Mom, I have a job interview in the morning."

What? That's my answer? Think, Steve, think. This was real. My father was gone.

"How about I drive directly to Idaho afterwards? It's an eight-hour drive, I'll get there a little after seven. I'll grab something to eat on my way."

"That's fine."

I exhaled.

"Mom," I said, "how did Dad die?"

"Heart attack while playing tennis. I'll tell you tomorrow."

I packed and mentally prepared for my Nike interview—an interview I would need to do even though I had just heard the worst news imaginable.

I was escorted into the office of Nike executive Del Hayes, a physically intimidating man of more than 300 pounds. He was sitting at his desk, where he looked to be reading my ultra-light resume. He looked up from the paper with a warm smile, stood for introductions, and I relaxed.

"So, you'd like to work for Nike?"

"Yes. I'm awaiting a decision if I can teach next year, but I'd rather work for Nike."

"Why?"

"Why?" I answered Del's question with the same question. "Great product, an Oregon brand. Many of my friends who work at Nike, in particular Mark Feig, encouraged me to apply. And I want to work overseas, which Feig says is a good possibility."

"It's true, we're looking for young people like you and Feig to work with the factories that produce our shoes. Would you move to Asia?"

"Absolutely. It's a dream of mine. My father is—er, was—

in the Air Force. Relocating has been my life." Talking about Dad in the past tense felt horrible, but I didn't think it was appropriate to explain at the time.

"I know you're married. Does your wife agree?"

"Yes, we've talked. We went to Germany to look for jobs, but it didn't work out. Feig is moving to Korea at the end of the year and we'd love to follow him."

"If you go to Asia, it would be in a year. You need time in Beaverton to learn about us, and we need to get to know you."

"That would be great!"

"What can you do?" asked Del, even though he had my resume. "Tell me about your college major."

"Math/computer science. I've been teaching/coaching for two years."

"We just bought a mainframe computer. Can you program it?"

"Sure, I programmed in Cobol and Fortran."

"How much do you make teaching?"

"Seven hundred and fifty per month, $850 including my coaching position."

I watched as Del wrote on my resume.

"How about $950 per month, six months programming the computer, six months in Product Testing, and then you move to Taiwan."

"Are you offering me a job?"

"When could you start?"

"Is two weeks OK?" I said, thinking that would give me time to deal with my father's death.

Del scribbled a final note and put down his pen.

"Done. Welcome to Nike! Follow me."

He led me to Carole Fields, who helped with the paperwork. When finished, she handed me Employee Identification Card #62, the number which didn't mean anything beyond some random numbering system. My date of hire was thirteen days later, 07-25-77.

"That's it?" I asked Carole incredulously.

"That's it. Report to Nick Parrish on your first day. He's your boss and will be expecting you."

I called Mary.

"Hey, I'm no longer a teacher," I said. "I'm now a computer programmer. We'll be moving to Taiwan in a year, starting at $950 a month!"

"Great news," she said. "Congrats!"

I drove east 500 miles on Interstate 84 to Mountain Home AFB. At the house, my mother saw me unloading my suitcase and came out to give me a big hug.

"How are you doing?" I asked.

"Much better than I expected. Come in, we'll talk."

"Better than you expected? What do you mean by that? I mean, Dad just died."

"Steve, your father prepared me for this. All military men are advised to prepare their wives of what to expect in case of a sudden death. Dad was trained in 'The Widow's Briefing' many years ago and he trained others. He briefed me several times over the years as things changed. I know just about everything that will happen."

I was surprised at how collected she was. Outside, I might have appeared the same; inside, I was a mess. I never had a briefing about what to expect.

"How about your finances?"

"I'm fine financially with our savings and Dad's military insurance. I'll get 55 percent of Dad's retirement pay. I'll start college in September, which I planned to do after he retired. It will just happen quicker than I expected."

"What can I do for the funeral?"

"Nothing. The Air Force is taking care of everything. They have contacted a funeral home near the National Cemetery in Dayton, Ohio, and will make all the arrangements. We just show up."

Above: In the 1971 district championships, which included teams from three Air Force-based schools in Spain and one in Morocco, I won the 800 meters by 15 seconds. Below: Our family was stationed at Torrejon AFB, Madrid, Spain in 1969-1970. Left to right, me; my dad, Steve; my mom, Joan; and my brother, Randy.

Above: Taking the victory stand in Nurenberg, Germany after winning the USDESEA Championship in 1:55.2, a new record. Right: Me with one of those "do-we-have-to-run-today?" looks on my face as a sophomore at the University of Oregon, 1973.

In 1975, as a senior, I led from start to finish in winning the 880 in 1:51.0 in a triangular meet with Oregon State and Washington at Hayward Field. The other Duck is Gary Sievers.

Top: Me, far left, at the 1972 US Olympic Trials at UO's Hayward Field. Dave Wottle (far right) tied the world record and later won gold in Munich. Above: Me en route to victory in the 880 (1:49.3.) at the 1974 Oregon State dual meet. UO's Mark Feig and OSU's Hailu Ebba, both friends of mine, on the left.

COME-FROM-BEHIND CHAMPION is Tennessee sophomore Willie Thomas, who sneaked through a crowd in the stretch to win the national title at 800 meters in 1:47.1. Narrowly-beaten also-rans in dramatic finish included Ron Phillips of Illinois (left), second by one-tenth of a second; and Northwestern's Tom Bach, who placed fourth in final.

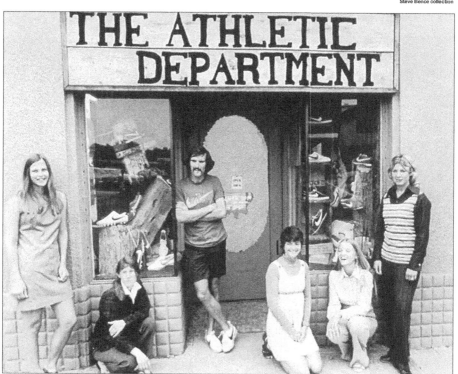

Top: Me, third from right, finishing sixth (1:47.7) in the 1972 NCAA Championship 800-meter finals at Hayward Field. Above: The employees at Nike's first store, in Eugene, during the 1972 Olympic Trials. Photo was taken just weeks after the Nike brand was officially launched. All competitors were welcomed at the Nike store, and would get a free tee-shirt with their name on the back.

Joan Bence

Just before Christmas 1974, my Mom—who was visiting me, along with my father, brother and grandmother—snapped this photo of a workout at Hayward Field. That's, left to right, Prefontaine, Knut Kvalheim, me, and Feig.

Top: In 1974, when Pre wanted to run a sub-4-minute mile in practice, more than a thousand fans showed up to help him do so. I (far right) did the pacing. Afterward, in the haze of field-burning smoke and back-dropped by the new West Grandstands under construction, he thanked the crowd. Above: In a 1973 intrasquad race, I beat Pre (just behind Geis) in a mile—sort of. Dellinger wanted Pre to run 2000 meters—so he essentially ran another lap, forever placing an asterisk on my "victory." Right: In 1974, Pre and Feig in their little-known hand-holding finish in a two-mile race in Corvallis.

They finally reached an agreement

Paul Geis and Steve Prefontaine deadlock in Corvallis two-mile

Top: In July 1974, I beat Ake Svensson, the Swedish national record holder, which made it easier to get into the big meets, in Vastervicks, Sweden. Time for 800 meters: 1:50.3. Above: My father, Steve, Mary and me fishing in Idaho shortly before his death. Right: Steve and Joan, my folks.

"Tell me more about how dad died."

"He had a heart attack while playing tennis after work. I don't know the details other than he got very tired, went to sit down on the bench, and the other players took him to the base hospital. He hadn't played tennis since he was in Thailand in 1974. He wasn't in pain and told the doctor he was just very tired. They thought it was a heat stroke; it was very hot yesterday. In the hospital, his heart stopped."

"How did you find out?"

"The corpsman called to ask me to come to the hospital and I sensed that Dad had died. On the drive over I prayed and told your dad that I released him. I was calm and composed by the time I arrived."

"I know how much dad liked to win," I said. "What was the score?"

"One of his playing partners said it was best three out of five, and they were in the fifth."

"So, 2-2 and in sudden death."

Mom burst out in laughter, knowing that Dad, with his sense of humor, would have expected nothing less.

"Yep," she said, topping me with her next line. "He played his heart out!"

We both laughed. Hey, it beat the alternative.

I drove home and arranged flights for Mary and myself to Ohio. Days later, a letter came from the Beaverton School District.

> Dear Mr. Bence: We have completed the interviews for the mathematics position at Mountain View School for which you were interviewed and wish to inform you that another person has been selected for the position.

I wasn't upset in the least. In fact, I felt relief in putting teaching behind me, at least for now. But, oh, what a month

July was turning out to be. Mary and I joined my mother, brother, and grandmother in Ohio.

It was easy to find where to go once we arrived at the cemetery; a makeshift shelter was set up with a small military detail. The service was about 20 minutes long, which included the playing of "Taps," a 21-gun salute from a rifle detail, and the folding of the American flag that had been draped over the casket. The flag was presented to my mother.

Afterward, I told Mom about my job with Nike.

"Nike?" she said. "What's that?"

"Athletic shoes. Phil Knight, a former Oregon runner, along with Bill Bowerman, started the company."

Mom's brow furrowed.

"Steve, you've got to let go of athletics now that you're out of college. What am I going to tell my friends? 'My son went through college so he could sell athletic shoes!' Please, can't you find a company that furnishes a product that everyone will buy?"

At Nike, I was the newest member of the small computer team that now numbered five—meaning, yes, at our main headquarters in Beaverton, we had fewer than half a dozen people on our "tech" team. By my estimate, the Beaverton office had fewer than a hundred employees.

My new boss, Nick, walked me through the office, introducing me to others with whom I would soon work. I learned that Nick sold the DEC mainframe computer to Nike, and Del Hayes hired him, the salesman, to get the system up-and-running. At the time, 1977, Nick predicted it would take ten years for Nike to outgrow the computer, but the data needs for our footwear business were already putting a strain on the system. Nick was tasked to plan out a digital growth strategy.

He gave me my first assignment, which proved to keep me plenty busy.

"Talk to Mike Walsh in Sales and see if you can help him.

He continuously asks for information and is never happy with what we give him."

When I asked Walsh for some of his time, he was eager to talk. "I need to know the inventory that I can sell immediately. I get pages of reports, but one day later they are out-of-date. I need information in real-time."

We had CRT terminals that could display real-time data; we just needed someone to program them for such. That, I realized, would be me. I worked with Walsh to map out the business process, prototyped some displays with test data, and worked with my small team to learn how to make it happen.

I turned to Rick, my co-worker on our small five-person tech team, who was the expert on the DEC computer, which was way beyond my pay grade. We brainstormed what was needed and Rick wrote all this complex code that I would copy-paste into my programs as subroutines. Shazam! Like magic, I would get the data needed to display on the terminal screens.

Rick spent most of his time at his desk in cowboy boots, at times leaning back in his chair, hands behind his head, with his feet propped up. "Most people think I'm not working," he said, "but I'm deep in thought in solving technical issues."

Who was I to doubt him? He did seem to solve problems and, as a newbie, I wasn't interested in getting inside his head. Computer folks are like hot dogs: you don't want to know what's inside them. Just enjoy the dog. In fact, I appreciated him for hiding the technical complexities of the computer stuff. We worked well as partners.

Before long I could walk through the office and see salespeople using the programs that we'd put together. Walsh said other sales locations were using them as well, and they seemed satisfied. Cool!

Soon after the start of the new year, and with our move to Taiwan still five months away, Feig moved to Korea and I took over his job in product testing. My new boss, Ron Nelson

(Nellie), was the first official Vice President of Nike Production. The product-testing job involved receiving samples from our R&D center in Exeter, New Hampshire, and from Nippon Rubber in Japan, which routed them through the Portland office of our Japanese trading company, Nissho Iwai.

Most of the R&D work focused on running shoes, and most samples were size 9, which I was told was Knight's size. It was convenient because I was that size, and I could often do an initial test myself, walking around the office and then going out on a run. With the many tests required, I had to find product testers both inside and outside of Nike, a pursuit that connected me to the local running community. Such runners were more than happy to be part of our shoe testing; in my five months in this job, I passed out hundreds of shoes to size-9 people in Portland.

Amid the testing, I was asked to be in a radio commercial entitled "I'm A Runner." Nike employees were often used in ads, catalogs, and commercials; it was more affordable and many of us were young enough and former athletes; the beer bellies and hair in our ears would come decades later.

For the radio ad, I ran behind a van on which a microphone was attached to a pole. They wanted to record my voice with the sounds of a quick-paced run, my feet striking the road in a rhythm with my breathing. Before the recording, I was asked to read the script.

"I'm a runner," I said. "I run every day, 365 days per year."

I stopped reading. "Hey, I don't run 365 days per year."

"It's not about you," said the director.

"I know, but runners need rest days. I can still hear Bowerman going on about his hard-easy philosophy, how—"

"Bence, relax. Right now, you're an actor; just read the damn script."

Nellie went the extra mile, introducing me to key people at Nike, including Tom "Jorgy" Jorgenson. He took me under his wing, often at a local bar where we'd go out for "a drink" after work and talk shop for hours. I learned more about the business and its people than I ever could from any sort of company handbook or tour.

"Join us for lunch," Nellie told me one day. "We're meeting in the parking lot at 11:45."

Eight people assembled, many of them top Nike execs, and I waited as we were paired up to reduce the number of cars. I was going with Jorgy.

"Watch Phil, he's going with Moodhe," Jorgy said. "This could be funny."

Jim Moodhe, the senior Salesperson, went to get his car as Phil stood patiently on the sidewalk. When Jim pulled up, Phil took the back seat on the passenger side, as if Moodhe were his personal chauffeur.

"Phil likes to play games with Moodhe," said Jorgy. "When Phil bought a car, Moodhe bought the same kind. When Phil got a dog, Moodhe got the same breed. Then Moodhe's dog passed away. The inside joke was, 'Thank God it wasn't Phil's dog because Moodhe would have to put his down.'"

We went to the Golden Crown restaurant for Chinese food and sat around the large, main round table. The conversations were spiced with humor, personal jabs, and inside jokes. This was a band of brothers and I could feel the friendship and trust among them. It reminded me of the strong relationships that I developed on the track team; the conversation was loud and boisterous.

I wondered whether I could ever become part of this inner circle. Sure, Nellie had invited me to this lunch, and I already had one-on-one personal relationships with half the people at the table. But I just didn't sense that I was ready. I was undeserving. I was an introvert. There was a fraternity element going on that "wasn't me," but, if I prepared myself as I had on the track team, and I could find my "event," —or, as Bowerman would say, my purpose—I realized I could score points for this team regardless of my introverted personality.

For now, I was content to be myself and sit back and observe. Maybe some day for the inner-circle stuff.

"Nellie, when are you going to get production under control?" Phil said out of the blue.

The comment landed like an incoming missile in the middle of the table. Phil sat back with a smile, like a spectator preparing to watch a good fight—that he'd provoked himself.

"Late deliveries, quality problems, pricing issues," Nellie countered. "Don't worry, we got this."

Seemingly satisfied, Phil turned to me.

"Bence, when are you moving to Taiwan?" Phil knew that I was following Feig to Asia that year, in mid-1978, to pave the trail that Phil had blazed in the 1960s and early '70s.

"June," I answered.

"Are you listening to this?"

I took that to mean that I was about to hear the closest thing to a job description that I would get, my marching orders—from the cofounder of the company himself.

"I'll give you the same advice as I've given to others," Phil said. He motioned me closer, as if a guru offering me life wisdom meant only for me.

"Don't ... fuck ... up."

Two months later, on a rainy June day, I settled into my seat on the plane, glanced at Mary, and took a few deep breaths. In twenty hours, we would be landing in Taipei. Getting ready to leave and saying our goodbyes had been hectic. It was all behind us now; there was nothing more we could do. I let go and enjoyed the moment of peace, then started thinking ahead.

Nike would take care of our living accommodations in Taiwan. We would find a house, be given an allowance for furniture, and be given a hardship bonus. Most of our belongings had gone into storage and we were asked to ship only clothing and the personal items that would make our house a home.

I turned to Mary. "You ready?"

She smiled. "No turning back now."

And the jet rose into the gray Oregon sky.

Mary Bence

In 1979, while living in Taiwan, I was asked to design a tennis shoe with a two-color outsole, Phil named it the Meadow—for Flushing Meadow in New York.

PART III
NINE

*Do not go where the path may lead.
Go instead where there is no path
and leave a trail.*

—Ralph Waldo Emerson

Chapter 11
Not in Kansas Anymore

When we arrived in Taipei in June 1978, the culture shock was like sticking your finger in a socket. The cabin door opened and we were hit with a blast of hot, humid air. Everywhere: people, people, people. Noise. Confusion. Frustration. We had to push our way to get a luggage cart and waited for nearly an hour before our baggage arrived. After getting through customs and immigration we found the Nike driver with a sign saying "Steve and Mary Bence." He helped us with our luggage, and had us stand on the crowded, filthy sidewalk as he ran to get the car. He took us to the apartment of Chris Walsh, the current General Manager.

Because of increasing labor costs and a shrinking pool of workers willing to work in a footwear factory, Taiwan and Korea were replacing Japan and the US for Nike production.

"Welcome to Taiwan!" Chris said, shaking my hand and offering a polite hug for Mary. "I thought it would be good for you to stay here, at least for a while. We can get to know each other and I can help you get oriented and find a house."

Chris's apartment was towards the top of one of the taller buildings in Taipei. Mary and I unpacked and settled in. A few days later I woke up about 2 a.m. to the sound of a picture swaying on the wall.

"Earthquake," I said, waking up Mary. I had lived in areas with frequent earthquakes before. Mary had not.

"Earthquake!!" Mary leaped out of the bed and headed towards the front door.

I followed. "Where you going?"

"To the elevator."

"No, that's the worst place to go. Let's stand here in the doorway until the building settles."

Mary settled as well. "Hey," she said turning to look at me, "we aren't in Oregon anymore."

The first year went fast. I worked with Chris to set up the new Nike Liaison Office. Phil Knight and a small leadership team were scheduled to visit in October 1978, and in August, with two months to go, we scrambled to have our grand opening when they were here.

Phil had started the process of setting up the office several years earlier, on an exploratory trip. He had come to Taiwan via an agent, Jerry Hsieh, who was a part of a family-run business called Mention Enterprises. Phil wanted more control over production, so he wanted his own Nike office to work directly with the factories, hiring Jerry to be the Vice General Manager. The General Manager position would be filled by a young, rotating group of Nike expats, myself among them. Jerry was the experienced local hand who would work with all of us. When Phil set up the liaison office, it was actually a subsidiary company named "Athena." The company structure would prove problematic down the road.

I developed personal and working relationships with the

top people in our factories, and began a weekly routine of meeting with them. Problems always came up, but with our diverse, strong global Nike team and with our factory people, we made great progress—in terms of price, quality, and delivery.

Mary had more difficulty than me adjusting to Taiwan because she was often home alone. I included her in dinners and events. She wasn't shy, so she would often show up at the office with treats for the office staff, creating a friendly family atmosphere.

The day came to say goodbye to my boss, Chris. I took over as the General Manager and welcomed my replacement-to-be, John Woodman, and his wife Kathy. Woody had been on the track team with me at Oregon. I didn't really know Woody; we first met my sophomore year at my apartment party. He was a three-year letterman in the high hurdles, having gone up against some of the best hurdlers in the US. For a while, he even trained with Guy Drut, the 1976 Olympic gold medalist.

The Woodmans moved into a house about 100 yards down the steep hill from our house in Yangmingshan, a hilly area between Taipei and the northwest coast of Taiwan.

"I am so glad you are here," Mary told Kathy. "I need someone more my age. Most of the American expats here are in their 40s, 50s, and 60s. They're very nice but more my parents' age."

The four of us quickly developed a deep relationship, something easy to do with fellow expatriates in a foreign country. It wasn't long before we were sharing intimate details of our lives.

The topic of children came up, and Kathy asked Mary, "Are you and Steve thinking about children?"

We were, and Mary let her know that we were open to adopting.

A year earlier, Walsh had helped Mary and me transition to life in Taiwan; now it was our turn to help Woody and Kathy.

"What should we know about this place?" asked Woody as the four of us strolled through an action-crazed snake alley where vendors called out to passersby, pointing to skinned snakes hanging, to snake blood, to cups of rice wine with various snake parts in them, and even to live snakes, some outside their cages. A red-light district was adjacent to the market. Local men would "get strong" drinking a cup of snake-penis wine and then visit a brothel. I was on edge; Mary hated snakes. Someone brushed by her and she about jumped into my arms.

"Tip One," I said to Woody. "Respect the people and local customs. You don't have to go native; in fact, you'd probably only make a fool of yourself trying. The locals know that you are American. They want to know and learn from us. You're a people person; just be yourself."

"It's OK if you want taste the snake or drink blood," said Mary, "but it's not OK to go down that side street."

We talked about the Yangmingshan area where we lived. It had the world's largest number of species of venomous snakes. They were released by the Japanese in spite, when they had to hand over the island to the Republic of China in 1945.

"So you're telling us we're not in Kansas—or even Beaverton—anymore, huh?" said Woody.

Obviously they were now learning what we had learned, echoing Mary's after-the-earthquake comment.

"Uh, yes," Mary said.

What I didn't tell Woody was that doing business here, though invigorating, had a dark side. Some of the local business practices—kickbacks and bribes, unethical or illegal in the States—were commonplace. I had adopted the philosophy that we would not behave as a Taiwanese company, rather as an American company located in Taiwan. As it turned out, we had a lesson coming in such regards—on-the-job training, as it were. And it would be a frightening lesson.

The Woodman/Bence friendship grew as we newcomers grew accustomed to a lifestyle far different from what any of us had experienced back home: we had company-provided houses, maids, and company-paid vacations. In addition, we each had a Nike-purchased car and driver; we weren't allowed to drive because of the dangerous, chaotic traffic in Taipei, although at times we would break the rule on weekends and on other rare occasions when traffic was light.

I told the Woodmans the story of Mary breaking the no-driving rule the previous October when Phil Knight, Del Hayes, and Ron Nelson had visited for the office opening. I had spent the afternoon with the trio at the Nike office and we had plans for dinner at one of the nicest Taipei restaurants, Alice's.

Mary had the car for the day, and let the driver go home early. She drove herself to the restaurant, parking a few blocks away, and took a taxi the rest of the way. She didn't want the top execs of the company to catch her driving; it would be a violation of an often-contentious rule.

At dinner, I was on my best professional behavior and nursed a beer. Nellie and the others were drinking double gin-and-tonics and ordered one for Mary, then a second, and a third.

After dinner, Nellie said, "Steve, what are you drinking?"

"Brandy."

"Brandy?"

Mary knew I was being a stiff, grabbed my glass, and downed it.

Nellie laughed and high-fived her. She turned to the others at the table and announced, "I'm no wuss." Boom, she'd gained immediate entry into the Nike fraternity.

"Hayes," Phil said, "I can't believe you're in the Orient."

"The drinks on the plane helped," Del replied.

Phil laughed. "Too many drinks. If it was possible to throw someone off the plane, they would have thrown us off."

After a bottle of the rot-gut Maotai, we called it an evening, and we watched our guests leave in taxis.

"That was fun." I said. "Where's the car?"

By then, she was starting to show the effects of her not being a wuss. Her brow furrowed and she had an "innocent uh-oh" look on her face, like Lucy Ricardo in an old "I Love Lucy" episode just before Ricky says, "LuuuuuuuuCeeeeeee!"

"Good question," she said.

We taxied home. I flew to the country's south with the Nike team the next morning to visit the factories and Mary found the car—eventually.

The year 1978 was a turning point for Nike manufacturing.

"Our factories in Taiwan and Korea are humming along," Phil said at the time. "Industry watchers point to our new factories, and our sales, and say we are unstoppable." Phil and his leadership were delighted with how everything was going.

When I arrived in Taiwan, I knew we had to focus on price, quality, delivery—and we did. But the job got bigger and the focus grew to Price, Quality, Delivery with capital letters. Solving problems required tracking down root-cause issues that led us to negotiating contracts with shipping companies, more engagement with key raw material suppliers, and a deeper understanding of the key drivers of cost in a pair of shoes.

We met with government officials, expanded the product development capability, shifted away from quality inspection to a quality audit, and searched for new factories to handle our growth.

Nike had only been in Taiwan for about three years. It was apparent that the country was quickly developing as a nation. Local labor was moving to more advanced products, and within five to ten years—just as happened in Japan—footwear manufacturing would have to move from Taiwan to other countries as well.

There was plenty of work to do; Woody and I divided up the responsibilities. "There's no play book," I told Woody.

"We've got to figure this out as we go."

I introduced him to my weekly routine. Tuesday afternoon we flew to Tainan, in southern Taiwan, to visit a factory named "Sheunn Yng" that Phil had sourced years earlier with its founder Ching Luh. Because it was a region where very little English was spoken, I made sure our Vice General Manager, Jerry Hsieh, would be there to translate. The factory primarily produced high-volume, low-end running shoes and offered little product development, so there usually wasn't much to talk about beyond the routine issues of the day.

We walked the production lines, spacious rooms designed for cutting, stitching, rubber making, stockfit, with all the parts coming together on a long conveyer belt where the uppers were lasted, and the bottoms attached. The product was inspected, put in a shoe box, which then went into a carton. There were more than 150 individual steps for a single pair of shoes, requiring about 500 workers to support one production line. A typical Taiwan factory had about four lines. The production process was like a symphony—everyone had to play their part just right. If not: disaster.

I liked to walk through the factory for several reasons. I wanted to stay familiar with the product being produced, look for any quality issues, and show respect to the workers. To get the quality that we needed, we selected the best factories we could find—ones with good working conditions and with senior managers who were easy to work with and aligned with Nike's values.

I saw a pair of SB4 shoes going down the production line and I pointed them out to Woody.

"Does that stand for Sub-Fours?" asked Woody. "As in a great time for the mile?"

"Nope, stands for Stephen Bence IV, my full name, although no one will know that—beyond you."

I explained. As a company, we listen to the voices of the

athlete in creating and producing performance product. It went back to Bowerman. I was an athlete, so I decided, why not? I'd create a shoe for myself. Take a chance; what's the worse that could happen?

I put together a "potato-head" shoe, picking parts from different models that resulted in what I considered a simple, lightweight, low-to-the-ground, cushioned, comfortable shoe. Since the shoes didn't require new tooling, and the simplified shoes would require less material and labor, they could be produced for under $5; that was peanuts compared to other low-end shoes, which ran in the $6-to-$7 range.

The factory made two pair of samples for me. I ran in one pair, and took the other pair back to Beaverton. I went through the office, showing the shoes to everyone I thought might be supportive. Curiously, there was no interest. None. I was told that there was no place in the product line for them. What was that saying about building a better mouse trap? I was learning that a new idea, even if good, needed to be sold. I wasn't a salesman, nor did I have the support of even a single respected leader.

On my last day in Beaverton, I decided to give it one last effort. I showed the shoes to Knight, knowing that if he said no, I'd wave the white flag of surrender. I could see Bowerman in my mind, glaring at me from the infield as I grinded down homestretch at Hayward.

"How much do they cost?" Phil asked.

"Under five, maybe four-seventy."

"Let's take a walk."

I followed him to Darrall Imhoff's office. Imhoff, 6'10", was in Sales, and was the answer to the trivia question about who guarded the Philadelphia Warriors' Wilt Chamberlain when he scored his record 100 points in a game against the New York Knicks in 1962.

"Imhoff," Phil said, "you've been complaining that we haven't come up with a shoe that you could sell as a $19.95

makeup."

Phil put the shoe on his desk.

"Here it is."

It was as if the Pope had blessed me.

Back in Taiwan, Woody and I spent the night in Tainan and had dinner with the Sheunn Yng people. Woody was so outgoing that we enjoyed being together with these folks even though we didn't speak each other's languages. Woody said it all as we walked back to the hotel in the calm warmth of the evening, chewing betel nuts and spitting the red juice on the sidewalk: "What do you think the people who graduated with business degrees are doing now?"

We both were living the dream. Woody had graduated with a degree in education but, like me, had worked at a Nike retail store while waiting for a teaching job to materialize. Now, we were both on a far different—and far more adventurous—trip.

The next morning we took the train bound for Taichung, where we would spend the night. We got off midway on the trip, in the city of Toulio, the rural area where the Feng Tay factory was located. We were picked up at the train station and taken to the factory.

"Is CH here?" I asked, entering the office area. Wang Chien-Hung was the founder of Feng Tay, having signed his Supply Agreement with Phil in November 1976.

"He's in a meeting," the receptionist told us, "but he's expecting you."

We walked into the room where CH was lecturing, loudly, to his top people in Chinese. It seemed so out of character for CH and so animated that it reminded me of a basketball coach too-intensely coaching his team, or a drill sergeant in the movies. Perhaps this was a holdover management style from the Japanese occupation. His people listened intently; almost "at attention."

"Woody, I've never seen him like this," I whispered, "maybe

we should wait in his office."

CH saw us out of the corner of his eye, turned, and immediately returned to his normal, friendly self.

"Hi," he said. "Just a couple minutes." Then, flipping on the light switch, he went right back to where he left off, reaming his senior managers as if that were the cultural norm—and it probably was.

We went to CH's humble office and I introduced Woody to him. After some small talk, Woody asked, "How did you get introduced to Nike?"

"It was late summertime 1976. Jerry Hsieh—he was one of my friends—called and said, 'There is a buyer who wants to visit you.' So the next day, Jerry and Phil came to my factory. This was the first time I met Mr. Knight. It took maybe twenty minutes to visit and they left. A couple of months later, in November, I got a Nike contract to sign. It was very simple."

"How has it been working with Nike?" Woody asked.

"Nike is easy to work with, friendly, and there is trust. I have four production lines. At first I gave one line to Nike. With big companies, it is hard to talk, difficult to get answers. With Nike I can talk directly to Chris Walsh and Steve. That's very easy for me. I like Nike's style of business."

"Any advice you have for me, the newcomer?"

"Nike people change a lot. There was Walsh, then Bence, and now you. Each person has a different philosophy and we must adapt. Nike is getting bigger, so more people are coming to our factory, and the Nike people don't always agree with each other. My advice for you, Woody, is you and I must work together to make sure communication is smooth; solve any personality problems or disagreements."

I understood, for the first time, that this Chinese management style might prove problematic as factories opened in other countries and other cultures. We walked through the factory and I saw another shoe that I had a hand in creating, a tennis shoe called the Meadow. When Phil Knight and his team had visited Feng Tay the previous October, CH showed him a two-color cup-sole shoe that he created for a brand in Europe. He was very proud that they were able to technically figure out to make an outsole that was more than a single color. CH offered it to Nike on the condition that we used the same last and outsole tooling. Nellie asked me to work with Feng Tay to make samples to send back to Beaverton with a quote on price.

I didn't know much about the sport, so I bought several tennis magazines and studied the shoes, especially the ads. I sketched out an upper for the shoe and Feng Tay made samples that I forwarded to Beaverton. It looked like a running shoe with a tennis bottom—extra material for toe drag, the best I could do—because I had only a runner's perspective.

A few weeks later, the news arrived via our office telex machine, an international communication system whereby messages arrived on a teleprinter: "The shoe is going in the product line. What's the name of it?"

"Athena," I responded, which was the name of our Taiwan office.

The next day, another telex arrived. "We're going with the name Meadow."

"Meadow?" I telexed back. "That's a stupid name. Who came up with that?"

"It's short for Flushing Meadow, an important US site for tennis in New York. Phil picked it."

"Hey, great choice! Love it!"

After a traditional Chinese lunch, Woody and I caught the train to Taichung where we visited the other three factories. I shared with him one of my painful early lessons about shipment dates. Nellie had asked if we could produce a late, large order for a retailer promotion; it had to be shipped by June 1 without impacting orders already in process. It was important to say no if it couldn't be done.

"Can we do it that fast, make that deadline?" I asked David Wang, President of Cheng Hsing, my main contact.

"No problem."

"Well, don't you need to check? Look at your production schedules? See if you can get the materials on time?"

David offered a slight smile, then his standard answer. "Steve, don't worry."

OK, whatever he said. I told Nellie "yes" and the order was placed.

Each week, David reported, "No problem. Don't worry."

Then, as the June 1 deadline was fast approaching, David's no-worries demeanor shifted.

"We have a problem. The order will be two weeks late."

With more than a little concern, I told Nellie the bad news.

"It's OK. I padded the June 1 date and it will be fine."

Lesson learned and passed on to Woody: try not to ask yes/no questions because, culturally, you'll always get a yes. We are the buyer, they are they seller, and they'll always want to please us. And, perhaps more importantly, always build in wiggle room, because things will go wrong.

Back in the office, in a conference room, all hell broke loose. Eight employees from the US were in Taiwan for training and would soon be assigned to work in Asia. Woody and I were giving a "Taiwan overview" the day before the group was to arrive at our factories.

Judy, an all-purpose employee, interrupted us. In the days before direct bank deposit, all employees were paid in cash with the largest denomination being NT$100 (New Taiwan Dollar), or about US$3. It took stacks of NT$ bills to cover payroll, which Judy dolled out from a cardboard box. When employees saw Judy, it was usually good news, but not today.

"It's Jerry Hsieh," she said to me. "He's here, demanding to talk with you. Says it's urgent."

This wasn't good. I'd recently had to fire the man. I walked into the office area and found an angry Jerry with four others: a policeman, a young kid, and two massive friends who appeared to be hired thugs. What the hell was going on? As it turned out, he had gone into his former office to find that Judy and her assistant, Grace, had taken over his space. He had taken the papers off Grace's desk and thrown them out the door of his former office. He was livid.

It wasn't because of tirades like this that I fired Jerry. He was a friend, calm, and critical for our success. It was something far more serious: we'd learned he was taking kickbacks from the factories. Years earlier, when Phil hired Jerry away from his family-run business, Jerry was offered a choice between commission-based compensation, or a salary of $50,000 per year. Jerry took the salary, huge in Taiwan at the time, and four times the amount I was making.

When Phil visited at the time of the 1978 Athena grand opening, he had a one-on-one conversation with Jerry, making it clear that kickbacks, or any secret commission-based compensation, would be grounds for termination. Jerry said he understood, but recently we'd heard he was violating that agreement. Jerry denied any wrongdoing. But an investigation produced factory receipts of such payments to Jerry—involving more than one factory, in fact. We had indisputable evidence.

After the firing, I had had the locks changed on the main door and to Jerry's office. It was shortly after that when he'd seen Judy and Grace in his office and had his meltdown. Teeth clenched, veins bulging, body sweating, he looked at me like a mad man.

"I am an Executive Shareholder of this company, and the action you took is illegal! I want the key to my office, and you must remove everyone and everything that isn't mine from there! If you think I'm wrong, you must first comply, and then go to court!"

I didn't know what to say. But Judy saved my butt. She'd had a good relationship with Jerry, and stepped in to explain—

in Chinese—our position. The more that Judy explained, the madder Jerry got. Suddenly he shouted something in Chinese and slammed his hand on a table, which scared the shit out of Judy. And, frankly, me.

Our attorney, Mrs. Ding, was on the phone and asked to talk to the policeman.

"This is a civil matter and police have jurisdiction over only criminal matters," Ding explained.

The policeman agreed and left.

The young kid that Jerry brought with him turned out to be a locksmith and Jerry told him to change the lock, but the kid was so intimidated he fled. It was obvious that it was impossible for Jerry to take back his office as if nothing happened. As the two thugs stood by, he packed up his personal belongings and they left without further incident.

The walk of Woody and I to the courtroom for our first hearing meant passing by a prison. I was able to see into a cell through a barred window. It was dark, with a concrete floor, bedding, and a filthy toilet. Did I need to be worried? I heard the Taiwan legal system was somewhat corrupt. Surely it was legal to fire Jerry, right? Or was I going to wind up in this place?

Woody and four others from our office were with me. Jerry was there with his attorney, a tough-looking guy, loud, animated, shouting in Chinese and pointing at me. Our lead attorney was named Mrs. Ding, a pleasant-sounding name. Jerry's attorney was Mr. Mung.

"Oh, no!" said the junior attorney assigned to us.

"What's he saying?" I asked, already starting to panic.

"Shhh. I'm listening. I'll tell you later."

Jerry, it turned out, had a legitimate case against us. When Phil had set up Athena, he needed a Taiwanese partner, which Jerry Hsieh became. Of the NT$500,000 needed to start the company, Jerry put in NT$100, a miniscule amount, but enough to give him part ownership. Legally, I could fire him as an employee, but that wasn't what the lawsuit was about. Since he was part-owner, I couldn't restrict him from the office. The result? Woody and I were being sued for having done so.

We turned to Rich Werschkul, Nike's lead attorney in Beaverton. Werschkul didn't know Taiwanese law so he sought out counsel from his legal buddies.

"I had drinks with a friend who knows how the legal system in Taiwan works," he told me. "You're right, it is a little corrupt. You need to find an attorney who has good connections."

"Did he offer any suggestions?" I asked, suddenly feeling very vulnerable.

"Not to worry," he said. "He gave me the name of just the guy, the best of the best. A 'Mr. Mung.'"

"Shit!" I said.

"What?"

"That's Jerry's attorney!"

The case went on for months, Woody and I were not in the country—on purpose—when the verdict came. It was a criminal case, and we were found guilty of illegally restricting access to Jerry, an owner of the company. But Werschkul worked his magic from Beaverton and there was no jail time for us.

Later, Phil asked me, "How's your good friend Jerry Hsieh?"

I told him the whole story.

"I was convicted," I told Phil.

"You were?" I was surprised that Phil didn't know.

"Yes, I was."

"What was the penalty?"

"Thirty days in jail or a fine. Werschkul handled it."

"Did he pay the fine?"

"Yes."

"Damn Werschkul," Phil laughed. "If he hadn't, it would have made for a better cocktail story—you and Woody in jail."

The Bences and Woodmans got into a routine of playing mahjong Sunday afternoons at our house, with gin and tonics. During one such session, the phone rang, a rare occurrence. Mary answered; it was a fellow American acquaintance. "The priest wants to meet with Steve and me," she said. "They don't have a phone at the church."

"You two must be in deep trouble," Woody joked. "You better go; we'll wait here until you get back."

The Catholic church, St. Christopher, was in Tianmu, a few miles down the hill from where we lived. It was led by a Dutch priest, Father White, who knew we were interested in adopting.

"I'd like to give you a tour of our orphanage," he said.

We furrowed our brows—or maybe only I did; Mary might have known more than she had led me to believe about the possibilities of adopting. Seemed like an odd request for this spur-of-the-moment call. Behind the church was a large area filled with children of all ages, most with obvious disabilities.

"When people have children that they can't care for, they bring them here," he said.

I looked around. It was heartbreaking The saddest situation was an older child, probably in his late teens, who was in a large crib with his wrists and ankles tied down, presumably to protect him against himself.

"With the healthy children, we try to adopt them to families. We have an infant girl who was supposed to go to a couple in the Netherlands, but they were rejected because they are too old."

We approached a small bedroom and were ushered in.

"This is Sister Margaret's room, and this is the baby who was scheduled to go to the Netherlands. Sister would like the baby to stay here; she has a huge heart, but she is too busy to take care of this child and I heard you might be interested in adopting."

It was true. Father White handed the baby to Mary.

"Can you take her?" he asked.

I was stunned. Mary bonded instantly. We were given time to discuss the possibilities alone. Father White returned.

"Well," he said, "what do you think?"

Mary nodded. "Yes, we'd like to adopt her."

He broke into a satisfying smile. "Do you want to take her now, or come back tomorrow?"

"Now is fine."

It was a bizarre moment, one of those shall-we-box-the-shoes-or-do-you-want-to-wear-them moments. Two hours ago we'd been playing cards with friends; now we were suddenly mother and father. With the baby in her arms, Mary's maternal instincts kicked in, and no one was going to rip that baby away. The Woodmans were still waiting at the house. On the way back, we stopped at a local store to buy supplies: baby bottle, formula, diapers—and more gin.

The store had a phone and Mary called the Woodmans to give them a heads-up. As we walked in the front door— me carrying a box of supplies, and Mary carrying the baby— Woody had his camera and caught the moment.

We propped up Lynn Margaret Bence in a chair next to the game table and finished playing. That night we emptied a wicker chest and made a bed out of it, which is where Lynn slept for her first night with her new parents.

So just like that, after interrupting our tile game, we were now a family of three.

Chapter 12
Say Hello, Say Goodbye

In June 1980, after my two-year assignment in Taiwan, I transferred to the Nike-owned factory in Saco, Maine, where I worked for less than a year. Del Hayes, who had hired me in 1977, ran the factory.

The story I heard was that Phil Knight sent Del to a shoe machinery auction at the recently shuttered factory in Saco. Phil instructed him, "Whatever you do, don't buy the building."

However, Exeter, New Hampshire was running out of manufacturing space with its growth in product development, Research and Development, and a Shoe University program for soon-to-be-Asia-expatriates.

The Saco building was dirt cheap, around $200,000, so Del bought the entire building. It turned out to be a wise purchase, but Phil wasn't so impressed.

"You bought the factory," Knight told him, "Now you go

start it up."

This was my introduction to shoe manufacturing in the US, and after my two years in Taiwan, frankly, I wasn't impressed. It operated within an antiquated New England shoe industry rife with adversarial relationships between us and the material vendors. Labor prices were high and making shoes was not a desirable US occupation.

The Plant Manager, more blustery than a Nor'easter, set the priority to hit a target production number every day that incentivized volume over all else. Bad idea.

The bulk of production was high-end running shoes that were developed at the Exeter facility. Among the models in production were the Yankee, Internationalist, Boston, Atlanta, Bermuda, and the new LDV. But the most important model was Nike's first "Air" shoe," the Tailwind. To keep the technology on a need-to-know basis, the Air units were manufactured in a separate, secure location—Building 108—Nike's version of the military's highly classified Area 51 in Nevada. The units were moved to the main factory for assembly.

Frank Rudy, the inventor of Air, would regularly go to Building 108 to watch his creation as it came to life. When he pulled into the parking lot, the dreaded message quickly circulated, "Frank's here!" Whether it was Frank or the R&D people from Exeter, the seasoned Saco production people clashed with the creative people. Saco's focus was on volume, period. Anything new just got in the way of "hitting the numbers."

What was happening in Exeter was, of course, open to interpretation; not everyone saw it like this. But my perspective suggested that the innovators wouldn't let go, always trying to make one last improvement even while the shoe was already in production—like chefs racing out of the restaurant's kitchen to put a dollop of sour cream on a new dish that a waiter almost had to the table.

Nike sales were growing rapidly, the result of new models

aimed at sports beyond running: court shoes and field sports, for example. Saco, it seemed to me, would never be able to keep pace with the changes and growth demands. As a result, the production of some of the Saco models were transferred to Asia. USA manufacturing could have worked—but only if Nike was content with a handful of running shoes with zero growth and rising costs per pair.

After less than a year in the very tactical day-to-day job at Saco, I was offered the opportunity to move to Korea, which I—with Mary's blessing—was quick to accept. Mary and I officially adopted Lynn, naturalized her, picked up her US passport, and moved to Busan.

The Korea liaison office was originally set up in Seoul, in the north of South Korea, which was the most comfortable living situation for expats, particularly because of the quality of schools. But the liaison office needed to move to the southern coast, closer to the factories. New expats moved directly to Busan, which we did, joining five others who were already there, and at least ten more coming soon.

Ross Blackman, the General Manager, stayed in Seoul to close the office while I took the title of Vice General Manager, leveraging my experience from Taiwan to gear up the new office in Busan. I knew Ross, an Aussie. He had been a long jumper on the UO track team, and competed in the 1974 Europe tour with Feig and me.

Many of the Korea nationals in the Seoul office didn't want to move to Busan, a less appealing city for living and a 250 mile commute to visit family and friends.

I caught up on the projected volumes, which were staggering. We needed a plan to get to a projection of 100 million pairs of shoes annually—an aggressive goal, to say the least. That meant roughly 170 production lines, the equivalent of 50 Saco factories, or 40 of the average-sized Taiwan factories I'd headed up.

The required capacity was doable in Busan, which had well over 500 total production lines, numbers reaching nearly a half-billion pair per year, the largest output in the world. Our job was to secure the production lines we needed and raise the factory capabilities to be able to produce high-quality performance sports footwear. The cavalry was on the way.

One hundred million pairs of shoes. I tried to wrap my head around that. Most of the shoes were sold in the US, which meant one pair for every three Americans. I remembered my mother telling me to "Work for a company that produced a product that most people would buy."

Turns out I now did.

I met with Whanil Jeong, who worked at one of the mammoth factories in Busan, in the Seoul office. Just as Phil hired Jerry Hsieh in Taiwan to guide us young Nike expats, Whanil was hired in Korea in that same role, with the additional role of handling Nike Asia shipping.

In telling just a couple of stories, Whanil broadened my understanding of the Nike connection in Korea. The first story made me laugh and the second made me proud.

"Nike visitors from Beaverton came to visit us," he began. "We went to a restaurant on the US military base, but only one car could enter the base. The Nike visitors pushed me into the car and I realized there were not enough seats for all of us. Two Nike people got into the car trunk. I was so surprised. Guess who they were?"

I shrugged my shoulders without a guess.

"Ron Nelson and, uh, Mr. Knight."

Whanil was shocked; this was a cultural taboo.

"Korean tradition doesn't allow a 27-year-old guy to sit in the car with his bosses in the trunk. I thought this might be American style, but I found out it's Nike culture. I like it, and respect it very much."

I laughed. Whanil continued to his next story.

"I married six months after joining Nike. I was just an employee, but it felt like family. We invited each other to dinner, to Jim Gorman's house, to my house. On my wedding day they came: Jim, his wife Gloria in Korean dress, and Mark Feig. It was very much a family-like atmosphere. Nike is the only brand for me; it is my life."

With Nike's help, Whanil started his own transportation company to support Nike's growing shipping requirements. TH Lee, from the same mammoth factory that Whanil came from, was hired to replace him in the new Busan office. I looked forward to working with him because of his deep wisdom and experience. TH already had a long history with Nike, which he was eager to share.

"In 1973, Mr. Knight visited our company and nobody knew who BRS was, nor who he was. I was available to spend five days with him so he could explain his plan for running shoes in Korea and how the factory can make it.

"I called in the factory designers, manufacturing experts, and Mr. Knight explained the concept of nylon running shoes. The technicians said they couldn't make it, that it couldn't be a good shoe. It was completely a new concept. At the time, Korea was making cheap canvas shoes with a rubber outsole."

Four years passed. The factories studied more. The first production of athletic shoes came from Korea in November 1977, a year after Taiwan.

It had been eight years since Phil's initial visit, and now Korea would become Nike's major manufacturing source of shoes. I was impressed with Phil's vision, patience, and persistence; it was definitely more than dumb luck. It takes time to change an industry.

Soon after TH was hired, Nellie called about the build-up in Busan. He said that he was sending a bunch of young people, some fresh out of college. Korea would be an on-the-job training center. They wouldn't all stay in Korea; some would go to Thailand, China, and other locations.

If the newbies struggled, if their egos or arrogance offended the local people or they weren't team players, boom, they were to be sent back to the US. TH was asked to connect with the factory management and be ready to settle any problems.

Ellen Devlin, in Product Development, came to Korea to work on her projects. We became friends. Like me, Ellen was a half-miler at Oregon, part of the first wave of young women to benefit from Title IX, the 1972 federal law mandating equal opportunities for women at federally funded institutes. Although a few years younger than me, Ellen had been coached by Bowerman after her collegiate career and had worked in Bowerman's Eugene lab before moving to Beaverton.

Early on, while working with the heads of factories, Ellen reported facing resistance; it was as if the factory employees were hesitant to allow her to be their boss. I met for lunch with one of the factory managers to help figure out the disconnect.

"I want you to understand Korean management style," he said to me. "All Korean men must serve in the military, so the business management style is similar. Very strict and we must follow orders."

"I can understand that," I said. "I see factory managers wearing jackets showing their rank."

"Yes, in Korea, women don't go into the military and they don't have high position in business. My managers want to know from you: Do they have to follow Ellen's instruction?"

That was simple. "Yes. Treat her the same as you would any other Nike developer."

"In Korea, we understand man, we understand woman, but we don't understand American woman."

"Well," I said, "it's time to learn."

Most of the Korean factories we approached were huge, twenty or thirty times the size of a typical Taiwanese factory, and they produced for more brands than just Nike. When we walked the production lines, not only did we see our Nike product, we also saw our competitors'. We heard talk of a Reebok aerobics shoe and then saw a production line in one of our factories producing the Reebok Freestyle, an all-white, supple leather shoe designed specifically for women.

"The shoe is crap," said one Nike employee. "The soft leather won't hold up."

Our experience with leather was in relation to shoes such as the Leather Cortez, basketball, and tennis shoes.

"They'll be getting a lot of defective returns from unhappy customers," said the employee.

Nike was criticized for taking a men's shoe, changing its color to pink or light blue, and calling it a women's shoe. Reebok's breakthrough in the women's market couldn't be this easy, could it? Over the months, that single Reebok line of production went to two lines, then three, four, and eventually moved entirely to another building. That one shoe fueled an explosive growth.

The lesson for me was that we needed to be more accommodating in our quality standards. Consumers define quality. The leather for a men's size 15 basketball shoe needed to be sturdy. Meanwhile, women wanted leather that was supple and flexible, even if it wasn't as sturdy as a basketball shoe. Reebok figured it out, and we followed.

Nellie, our VP of Production, gave me a heads-up that he would call; it was another teachable moment. There was a problem with a shoe called the Jury, an all-black shoe for basketball referees. The shoes were making black marks on the basketball court and had to be recalled. I did my homework before the call on the black rubber; I was defensive.

"Nellie," I said, "the spec sheet from Beaverton said to use the same black rubber compound that we use on our running shoes, BRS 500."

We had recently improved the durability of our black outsole rubber compound. It was common for the outsoles to wear out quickly. Resoling or a patch with Shoe Goo extended the life of a shoe. The goal was to produce a running outsole that would last 500 miles; in making the compound, our chemists had applied lessons from the tire industry, but apparently overlooked the possibility of skid marks on indoor courts.

"Schools banned those running shoes from the basketball court for leaving black streaks, you know that," Nelson said.

This wasn't a blame-and-punish call, it would be a lesson—and I'd heard a few of those before. For example, Nellie had told me that it wasn't our job to say "no" to a designer. Our job was to understand what the designer wanted, and work together to find a solution.

"The developers in Beaverton don't know what you in Asia know," he said. "You need to watch out for these mistakes."

My definition of quality just expanded again. Instead of making sure the factory followed the Beaverton specs, we needed to understand the end-consumer, in this case basketball referees, and make the corrections so we didn't have mistakes like this in the future.

I passed along the message. No skid marks! It was a continuation of the message to remain open-minded and look through the lens of a consumer or a designer, not just our own production view.

In November 1982, Mom visited us in Korea for just over a month. Because she was a widow with military benefits, she could go to the base commissary and buy groceries that we couldn't get on the local market. Beer was rationed and she bought her full allowance for us.

By now, just over two years since we adopted Lynn, Mary

and I felt ready to adopt a second child. Mary did the research. She went to the Holt International Adoption Agency, which handled the process of Americans adopting Korean orphans. (Interestingly, Holt was based in Eugene, where, in years to come, cofounder Bertha Holt would hold the Masters record for the 400 meters for women 90 and older!)

"Steve and I have an adopted girl from Taiwan," Mary told the Holt representative, "and we are interested in adopting a second child here in Korea."

"Do you have the child yet?"

"No, that's why I'm coming to you."

"I'm sorry, but we handle adoptions to the US, not for here in Korea. You find a child to adopt, and then we can help you."

"How do I do that?"

"Go to an orphanage. There are many in the Busan area."

With my mother visiting, Mary had Mom join her on visits to the local orphanages. Afterward, the two were heartbroken.

"There are so many orphans, all ages," Mary said. "We want to help them all."

"Did you narrow it down?" I asked.

"There was an orphanage with a one-year-old boy who caught my attention and a room full of infants. We can go there and decide together."

A few days later, I walked through the orphanage, which consisted of six large rooms. Each room had about ten children, all about the same age. We went to the room with the one-year old, then the room filled with cribs and infants. It seemed like a pet store, as if we were picking out a dog. We decided on a 10-week-old girl, named her Kelly Anne Bence, and brought her home. Holt helped us finalize all the legal requirements with the US. I thought of the many legal hoops that families had to go through to adopt; we had it easy!

Our family of three had now grown to four.

Busan was modernizing quickly. At the peak of Korea production, about a billion Nike dollars per year went into the local economy, plus the money from other brands who sourced
production there. The city was transforming into something
almost unrecognizable.

It's amazing how many economies around the world started with apparel and footwear, which then became catalysts for
broader industrialization for those countries. I saw it happen
real-time in Busan. Factory jobs were becoming "my parents'
job." Younger, more educated Koreans were not interested in
production work in a shoe factory.

As in Taiwan, the production of footwear was moving out
of Korea. We knew Nike would have to move on. As happened
in Japan, these two countries were becoming first-world countries. The Korean government recognized that there would be
problems if the shoe industry collapsed too quickly, putting
tens of thousands of workers out of jobs, so it subsidized the
large factories that were struggling to remain profitable, which
gave them and us some time to figure out what to do next.

I thought back to 1977 when I was hired by Del Hayes.
Ten years later I was about to move home, having lived in
Taiwan, Maine, Korea, Beaverton, and Korea again—ten jobs
and six international moves. After adopting the two girls,
Mary and I had two biological children of our own: son Chris,
born in Portland, and our youngest daughter, Cory, born in
Korea.

On New Year's Eve 1984, I reflected on the year and gave
it a perfect 10 out of 10 score. Chris had been born in May.
We had moved back to the states but, in 1986, it was back to
Korea.

I developed personal relationships to last a lifetime, and
had a role in building the foundation for Nike's future success.
I found meaning in my jobs and now looked forward to what
was next for me and our family of six.

The 1964 Tokyo Olympics marked the modernization of Japan, and the 1988 Seoul Olympics did the same for Korea. I realized that I had lived in both of those countries leading up to the two Olympics.

Sports, shoes, Asia, and family now defined me. And there was more to come—of each.

Chapter 13
The Rest of the World

In 1987 we moved back to Beaverton for good. Mary and I were 33 years old, our children now 1, 3, 5, and 7. We weren't as mobile as we were "before kids," and we didn't want to move them every couple of years.

If I'd been a military field captain on the ground in Asia, fighting the good war for Nike, I was now amongst the Pentagon bureaucrats. In Asia we would decide and go; in Beaverton, it was *decide, decide, decide.* I quickly discovered the way to get things done was via meetings. And I found myself having a meeting just to figure out which meetings I needed to set up.

I was asked to lead the startup of our Footwear Materials group, which I set up to run like a liaison office in Asia. The difference: instead of working with our Tier 1 factories that produced the finished product, my team in Beaverton would work with selected Tier 2 factories, those that provided raw materials for the Tier 1 factories. The main vendors included Nike air bags produced in Beaverton, synthetic leather out of Japan, full-grain leather from Prime Tanning in the US, spike plates from Germany, and several commodity materials where we could negotiate lower prices based on our large volumes.

My team set direction, negotiated prices, established volume contracts, and gave production forecasts. The Tier 1 factories continued to purchase directly from the Tier 2 vendors.

The most important part of the job was to establish personal relationships with the vendors. There were always challenges and problems to be solved, and adversarial relationships made things worse. We had two main synthetic leather vendors in Japan, Teijin Cordley and Clarino. Clarino had an American sales rep, Tim Anderson, who worked with Jacquie Bergstrom on my team. They worked well together, so well that I later joked they overachieved when they married.

I chose to manage the existing relationship that I had with Millard Freeman, with whom I'd worked in Maine. He was about 60 years old, a grumpy, lovable, seasoned New England shoe dog. When the Maine factory shut down, air bag production was moved to Beaverton, and Millard moved across the country to run the factory. I worked with him as I would with any of our Tier 2 vendors.

"Millard, this is big," I informed him. "The forecast is going from about a million pair per month to 3 million."

"OK, thanks Steve," he said. "But I'm not tripling capacity based on your forecast."

I went to my boss, Dave Taylor, nicknamed DT. He was a four-time all-American distance runner at UO, two years behind me, and in the UO Sports Hall of Fame. DT had worked in New Hampshire, the Philippines, and Taiwan before taking over the Production VP role in Beaverton.

DT joined me at my next meeting to help convince Millard that the dramatic forecasted increase was real. New air shoes were in development and the forecasts were beyond big.

"Steve's forecasts never match the orders we get," Millard told DT. "One month it's over, the next month under. Steve says on average, it's right. I've told him, 'It's like I have one foot in scalding hot water, and the other foot in freezing cold,' and Steve says on average it's room temperature. I don't want to react to a forecast, I want real orders; then I'll adjust."

"Then adjust," Dave told him. "It's true, you need to triple capacity, expand the production space, bring in additional equipment, and hire more people. It will be on me if the increase doesn't happen."

Millard reluctantly followed through. Within six months, orders for air had tripled. And product was delivered on time.

I was getting bored with my job, continuing to do what I was doing for the past ten, now almost twelve years. I didn't want to leave Nike; my personal identity, for better or worse, was too attached. I decided to get my MBA to develop a business acumen on top of my international experience.

As fate would have it, DT asked if I wanted to apply for the University of Oregon Executive MBA program. Nike was a sponsor but didn't have a Nike employee enrolled. Perfect timing. Along with four others, I applied. Nike let the UO decide which candidate to accept. After Nike reviewed our GMAT test scores, perused our resumes, and did interviews, I was selected for the two-year program that the company paid for.

Classes alternated all-day Fridays and Saturdays at a location within a few miles of the Nike campus. It was intense; in fact, there was a workshop devoted soley to preparing us for how to juggle a full-time job, full-time Master's program, and family life.

After graduation in 1991, I started down a path of business process improvement and transition management. In the twenty years since Nike's 1972 birth, it had grown to be a $3 billion company, taking on all the problems that come with such rapid success. No one designed how Nike worked; it just happened, so there were plenty of problems—or, if you're an optimist like me—opportunities for improvement.

In 1992, Nike's 20th birthday, I reflected on my fifteen years at Nike. By my count, we had produced footwear in 22 countries, and the 23rd, India, with its billion-plus population, had been identified as the next stop on the Nike tracks. India would turn out to be the last new Nike footwear manufacturing country identified for the next 30 years.

Since 1977, I had lived, visited, or in some way supported, all the countries except India. In the 1960s and 1970s, Japan and the USA were the key countries. Both had a mature footwear industry and developed into first-world nations.

Nike shoes were labor-intensive to make, requiring a shift to countries that had well-established footwear industries, low-cost labor, and plenty of willing workers. Knight had chosen Taiwan and Korea as our next manufacturing locations. By 1992, of the 100 million Nikes produced annually, two of three were coming from these two countries.

Nike was on a fast pace of growth in the 1990s, hoping to double production to 200 million by 2000. But the decade was marked by turbulence in some countries we'd expanded to—even as we realized we couldn't return to the countries that had got us here. At times, we were between the proverbial rock and a hard place.

Some countries, such as Guatemala, came-and-went. In the mid 1980s I went on a factory visit; the country was producing a small number of Nike shoes. A driver picked me up at the airport in a bullet-proof car; he had a handgun and a rifle. I learned the factory president had been kidnapped and held captive until a ransom was paid, apparently a common practice in Central America, and this armored car was a deterrent for it happening again.

Above: Mark Feig, Mary, and I at our wedding. We wanted a picture similar to the one from Butch Cassidy and the Sundance Kid. *(Paul Newman, Robert Redford, and Katharine Ross). Below: Groomsmen, left to right, Gary Sievers, Mike Long, me, Feig, Pat Tyson—all UO runners— and Mary's younger brother, Mark Jacko.*

Top: In Taiwan, in 1978, we were welcomed at the Sheunn Yng factory by a sign out front. Above: My mom, Joan, visited us in Korea in November 1982. That's Lynn on my shoulders.

John Woodman

In Yangmingshan, Taiwan, we interrupted a game of mahjong with the Woodmans to go see a priest, who wanted us to meet someone. When we arrived back at the house, we had a new daughter, Lynn, Woody took our picture as we came in the front door. Now that we were "instant parents," we'd stopped at the store to buy baby supplies.

Steve Bence collection

Steve Bence collection

Steve Bence collection

Top: In 1984, in Eugene, we got to meet Bertha Holt, whose organization helped us with our adoption in Korea. Left to right, Kelly, Mary, Lynn, Chris, and Bertha. Above left: Whanil Jeong and YC Park founded two major factory groups in Korea in the 1980s that Nike continues to utilize today. Above right: Me speaking at a Korea celebration in 1982. Two of our factory partners are on the right.

Top: In 2005, my son Chris, at the time an engineering student at Purdue, and a friend, Brandon Sargent (striped shirt), joined me in China for a factory tour. Note the "Bowerman" badge on a worker's shoulder, signifying this was a speciality product line. Above: After giving up running, I joined a walking team for the Hood to Coast Race. In 2014, this was our T-Wrecks team, which competed in the Corporate Masters+ division. It included some of the most tenured employees at Nike, many now retired.

Top: Our lifelong friends, the Woodmans and Taylors at Sunriver in 2006 for Kelsey Woodman's wedding. Left to right, John Woodman, Kari Woodman Warner, Kathy Woodman, Kelsey Woodman Buchanan, Kyle Woodman, Katie Woodman, Lynn Bence, Kelly Bence, Chris Bence, Cory Bence, Lisa Taylor Rosenfeld, Mary Bence, me, Terry Taylor, Dave Taylor. Above left, in 2008, at one of Nike's "Heritage" tours at Hayward Field. That's me and Kenny Moore flanking the Bowerman statue with Pat Tyson in front. Above right: In 2019, with the Duck mascot at the UO's Jane Sanders softball field, which we used for the Nike tours while Hayward Field was being redone.

Top: Without Limits *producer Tom Cruise at the 1998 premiere in Eugene. Wife Mary and daughter Cory, front left, photo-bombed it. Not a Photoshop job! Above: In 2004, I, top right, gathered with Nike colleagues John Woodman, back left, Geoff Hollister, front left, Tinker Hatfield, middle, and my former UO track and field coach, Bill Dellinger, at Nike Nationals, a high school cross-country event we sponsored in Portland.*

Top: In 2018, I took one of our larger Nike Heritage tours to see Pre's Rock, at which he died in 1975. Above: In 2021, Mary and I at the new Hayward Field, which I love.

If this was meant to make me feel safe, it wasn't working.

I met with the factory president and his senior people in his conference room. Ten minutes into the meeting, his secretary came in and whispered something to him. He seemed alarmed and immediately left. He returned some fifteen minutes later.

"Everything OK?" I asked.

"It's fine," he answered. "There was a bloodless military coup at the capitol and my children's school is nearby. They're all safe."

My eyebrows instinctively popped up. But we continued the meeting, including the factory tour, as though nothing had happened.

Nike contacted Mary at home to tell her that I was safe, even though neither of us knew that I was in any danger. In fact, when I got back to the hotel, I intentionally went for a run by the capitol and didn't see anything out of the ordinary. For a multitude of reasons, including political instability, we dropped Guatemala as a candidate for long-term Nike manufacturing.

We tried other countries: Mexico multiple times, Ireland, UK, Spain, Chile, South Africa, and New Zealand with varying degrees of success.

Another factory visit for me was to Borovo, Yugoslavia, the location of a factory making shoes predominantly, if not exclusively, for Europe. It was an unremarkable facility that seemed to have its niche. I later learned that it had been destroyed in the '90s during the Yugoslav Wars—first in Croatia and then in Bosnia and Herzegovina—that led to the breakup of the country.

Several countries had a proven long-term, although minor, role in the big Nike picture: Brazil, Argentina, and Italy. Additionally, several countries—Malaysia, the Philippines and Thailand—seemed to have the potential to be long-term production sources but didn't pan out as such. Thailand probably peaked at about 20 percent of total annual production, the Philippines much less. Both were developing countries and once they developed to a certain point, it was time for Nike to move on. Because of their inability to attract workers, they weren't capable of growing with us.

Given all this, where, possibly, could we turn to meet the demand? China, Phil decided. Population? More than one *billion* people, the largest country in the world, nearly three times the size of the US.

In the early 1980s, China opened to the world. It was a communist, undeveloped country, and had no modern footwear industry at all. But Phil believed strongly it could be the next major source for our shoe production if we could be patient and persistent. He backed up his belief by sending a small Nike team into the country to work with government officials in getting a factory started.

Steve Roth and Rick Lower were part of the first team going into China. They had worked at the R&D facility in New Hampshire when I was at our factory in Maine; we worked together in Korea, and were fellow runners. I knew them well; but could they pull this off—this move to China?

China was complex. It would be like juggling six chain saws—in the dark. Lots of moving parts. No precedents. No context. Woody had thought Taiwan was hard with no playbook; this was ten times harder, maybe even more. And Nike didn't like to fail.

In years to come, there would be a Harvard Business Case study about Nike setting up shop in China—but the case study focused on how *not* to start up in China. We made mistakes, but, obviously, those doing the bushwhacking eventually figured it out.

"It was a bold move," Lower told me. "A lot of people were skeptical."

Some thought it was simply too big of a jump. And, in some ways, they were right.

"It was a struggle for over five years," said Lower.

Goals were set. Goals weren't met.

"But," said Lower, "Phil never wavered."

Said Roth, "Imagine going into an empty building which just got electricity. We had to bring in the machines, teach the workers how to make shoes. We could only take this project so far."

The political climate started to change. The only way that we were going to be successful in China was to introduce Taiwanese factory management, not easy to do because it being illegal for Taiwan citizens to visit mainland China. Phil asked CH Wang, the founder of Feng Tay in Taiwan, to consider producing in China. With special China government approval, Roth toured CH around Fujian Province, where he picked the city of Putian, only 140 miles across the strait from Taiwan.

"Some thought it would be difficult for the Taiwanese to work with mainland Chinese," said DT. "It turned out to be easy because, ethnically and culturally, they're pretty much the same."

By 1992 China was about 10 percent of Nike's production and would grow to around 50 percent within the decade. The blueprint was set to close down production in the declining countries as we, together, simultaneously opened factories in the countries targeted for growth.

Whanil Jeong, the founder of the Chang Shin factory in Korea, jumped in with both feet—and nearly drowned.

"I opened two factories at the same time, one in China and one in Vietnam," Whanil said. "I was in financial trouble. The Korean banks closed their doors on me. I went to Beaverton to borrow money—$5 million—and DT said yes. Nike trusts me." It was paid back in only two years.

CH Wang was more careful as he expanded into Vietnam. He made sure that China was running smoothly before he moved his management team from there, and it didn't hurt his operations.

There was tension in the Vietnamese factories; I surmised it was the cultural differences between the Taiwanese and Korean management styles overseeing Vietnamese workers.

Indonesia was next. Woody had been the GM in Taiwan, and Thailand, and was now the first GM in Indonesia. He set up the Nike office in Jakarta, working with the six companies making our shoes.

Just as the tensions were rising in Vietnam—and probably for the same reasons—it wasn't long before Woody was taking the heat for the working conditions in the Indonesia factories.

"We feel the workers employed are better off than before they started producing Nike shoes," Woody told US reporters, "better off than they would be without those jobs. It is difficult for First World people to understand this if they don't understand Third World economics. I know of the labor disturbances in the factories, and I trust that the factory management will solve them."

Woody expressed what most of us expats believed at the time. The press called it the Ostrich Defense; we called it the truth. In any case, Nike was becoming a lightning rod for critics; we became an inviting target for the labor problems in Asia that weren't of our making.

In 1998, Phil went to Washington, D.C., to address—in a sort of Daniel-in-the-Lion's-Den setup—the National Press Club. He owned the problem and said Nike would raise the minimum wage for its workers and impose American air-quality standards on its plants overseas.

After the speech, the *Washington Post* reported: "Phil Knight was remarkably candid during a speech this week at the National Press Club in acknowledging how much damage the critics had done to his company's image."

Phil wasn't just talking; he was committed to making improvements. I noticed that more and more people who previously were pointing fingers at Nike were now employed at

Nike. Phil was taking ownership. Just Do It, Phil, I wanted to say. That Press Club speech marked a turning point for Nike.

And yet the factory workers story wasn't going away. In spring 2000, a group of University of Oregon students held a sit-in at the school's administrative offices to protest the university's unwillingness to support a student-led organization called the Workers Rights Consortium. The WRC complained that companies like Nike were exploiting Third World workers. Phil countered that he didn't believe the WRC was seeing the whole picture and encouraged colleges to not join the organization. UO President Dave Frohnmayer found himself between a rock and a hard place, but ultimately chose to join. Phil was wounded deeply. He saw it as rebuffing of the very company that had helped the university in so many ways—and a too-narrow view of what was going on in Nike's factories. He turned his back—and closed his wallet—on his alma mater. And I couldn't blame him.

He valued relationships, especially with UO students, some of whom he'd angered, even if I think it was misplaced anger. Nike hadn't created the conditions in the Asia factories, but I know we improved them, especially after Phil took the lead to do so in 1998.

In fall 2000, Phil invited our family to join him in his skybox at Autzen Stadium. When we arrived at the box, he asked, "Did you see the students handing out leaflets?"

The students were protesting Nike; Phil was clearly concerned—and hurt.

"Yeah, there were students on the corner," I answered.

"Go down and get a leaflet. I'd like to see one."

On the way back I read it.

"What does it say?" he asked as I handed it to him.

"That Nike workers are overworked, underpaid, and having to put up with poor working conditions."

"That could describe you," he said, smiling. But I knew

deep down it bothered him.

Just because a company is large and successful doesn't mean it's exploiting people to get to the head of the pack. Though not perfect, Nike's factories treated its people well—and went out of its way to treat them even better after Phil's ballsy appearance at the National Press Club.

As a UO grad myself, I was grieved when Phil felt it necessary to sever his relationship with the university, though I understand why he did what he did. He had no other choice. That said, I was also thrilled when the university's attorney discovered that belonging to the WRC opened the UO to all sorts of liabilities, convincing Frohnmayer, in October 2000, to pull out. With that, Phil happily rejoined the flock.

Undoubtedly, Phil Knight wielded power with the UO. I didn't take his side on such issues because of his power but because his of thinking. He was right to rebuff the UO when it had clearly rebuffed him—and he was right four years later when he questioned Bill Dellinger's replacement as UO's track and field coach, Martin Smith.

After Smith had been on the job five years, Knight wasn't the only one who thought the coach wasn't doing enough to maintain Oregon's distance-running tradition. A bunch of us who'd run at Oregon agreed. We called ourselves The Lame Ducks and we would pass the hat every year to raise scholarship money for the track and field program, somewhere in the range of $50,000 to $100,000, which Phil matched. (For those who think Phil demands that Nike people follow his lead, he stopped his Lame Ducks money match during the WRC controversy but encouraged us to continue giving as we saw fit.)

Like Phil, we wanted more emphasis on Track Town USA, an extensive home schedule, big national meets, and a program that honored UO's traditions of excellence in the middle distances and distances.

Smith was on a different page. It appeared his approach was sending athletes around the country to big meets so they could get fast times, but we fans got the short end of that stick. In 2004, I believe there was only one sub-4-minute mile run in the state of Oregon, done on the Nike campus, not in Eugene; it came when we staged a mile run to celebrate the 50-year anniversary of Roger Bannister first breaking the 4-minute barrier. In those fifty years, 27 UO runners ran under four minutes, only one during Smith's tenure.

When Athletic Director Bill Moos let Smith go in 2005, it was a win-win: UO got what it wanted, a return to its distance tradition under former Stanford Coach Vin Lananna, and Smith got what he wanted: Oklahoma, a program that was happy to let him chart his own course.

Amid such controversies involving the UO, my work had shifted to implementing large business process changes and new IT solutions, which included all our factories. In 2003, I began helping people with transition management, which involved job changes, communication, and training.

In the early years the question at Nike had been, "Where do we go next?" Now, the question wasn't so much "where" but "how." And that all boiled down to people.

At its essence, Nike is about the hundreds-of-thousands of individuals who come together to produce great shoes. One of my most memorable conversation was with a young product developer, Yoonie Yoon, at Whanil's company, Chang Shin, in Busan.

"Tell me about your job and what you like about it," I said to her.

"When I'm given a project, I receive a thing called ITP, Initial Tech Package. It has all the sketches, technology, and the concept that the Nike Beaverton World Headquarters team wants to put in the shoe."

She shook her head in obvious frustration. "Usually when I look, I've never seen anything like it. They want me to do this and put it in a shoe. How am I going to do that? After a lot of trials and meetings, in the end, I see the results. Wow, this is what they wanted to begin with!"

Her mood turned from angst to amazement. "We have the same goal as a team, Nike and factory, even though we are on the opposite sides of the world. It is amazing what can be done. And at the end of the day, I'm happy and thankful that I'm part of this whole process. When I see that shoe in the market, it gives me emotions because it's not only beautiful, but I know the things behind the scenes. It gives me goose bumps. That is what keeps me going with this job."

I was struck by how excited she was, and the importance she had in bringing a product to life. Beaverton often comes up with the idea, Korea and Taiwan translate that into a shoe, and the manufacturing countries take that single pair and produce a million in a full size range, sold in more than 160 different countries.

Nike, I realized, was in good hands with this younger generation.

Chapter 14
Hood to Coast

To this point, I've written about my running experience at Oregon, and my Nike experiences around the world. But no such personal perspective, based on Nike and on running, would be complete if I didn't write about Hood to Coast (HTC). I've always considered Nike's story to be a twining of two narratives: one the fairly serious retelling of how and where we built shoes; the other a fairly lighthearted retelling of how and where we blew off steam, acted crazy, and drank a wee-bit too much. So, what follows are my HTC memories.

It was 1985 and I was back in the states, doing things I couldn't do oversees: watching live sports on television and recently released movies in theaters. Bo Jackson won the Heisman, and we were still talking about Eddie Murphy's performance in Beverly Hills Cop.

Mike Franklin, the team captain for an HTC team called

Tarahumara found my office.

"Steve, do you have a few minutes to talk about Hood to Coast?"

"Come in, I'm catching up with what I've missed."

He explained how the event had been started several years earlier by a former Oregon athlete, Bob Foote. The event consisted of eleven-person teams running the 165 miles from Mt. Hood to Pacific City on the Oregon Coast. It had started in 1982 with eight teams, expanded to 64 teams the following year, and 150 teams the third year.

"Wow, 165 miles!" I said. "How long does that take?"

"In the 17-hour range. We entered a Nike team in the second year, a mixed team of five women and six men. We rented a Winnebago, stocked it with beer, and basically had an all-night party. We didn't care about how fast we ran—and we finished dead last."

I did the math. "So, each of the eleven runners runs about 15 miles?"

"Not all at once. We each run three times, so it is an average of five miles per leg."

"Doesn't sound like much fun to me."

"Stay with me," he said. "Last year we entered again; there was a newly created corporate division. We won it."

Hmm. Now it sounded fun to me. It was a little like the Civil War relay. I understood their original goal was just an excuse to party. However, they had gotten a taste of winning, and their goal had changed.

"Want to be part of it?" he asked, reminding me of me when I asked Pre to join our Great Race Team against the Beavers.

"Count me in."

Mike's role would turn from party host to team captain. I trained the next few months for my three legs, raced hard, and Tarahumara won the division for a second year in a row.

I loved the event; it was me—*running, competitive,* and *team.* It was surreal running three times over a 17-hour period.

We started the race at Timberline Lodge, 6,000 feet in elevation, worked our way down to Portland, crossed the Willamette River, then continued west through the suburbs, the forest, farmlands, up and over the coastal range on back roads, and finished on the beach at Pacific City.

The time went fast, and we slept when and wherever we could. It was like a one-day moveable feast of running wherein you had to test yourself on the road, in one of the two vans that carried about half a dozen people. Your mind quickly becomes fuzzy from the running, the lack of sleep, the logistical headaches. All while trying to beat the thousands of folks doing the same thing. It was crazy.

I enjoyed the first leg, running down the steep, winding road from Timberline Lodge. I relaxed going down the mountain, taking my long half-miler strides, and let gravity do its thing. I ran again in 1986, and we won again for a three-peat.

And then it happened: the streak ended. In 1987, we finished second. Mike figured out who had beaten us—and why.

"Hewlett-Packard," he said, "brought in runners from around the country for a team-building event."

We averaged 7:11 per mile, our slowest time yet. Did we have fun?

"Losing isn't fun," said one team member.

"Second place is the first loser," said another.

OK, I was convinced. Soon, Mike's job required him to move on, so I took his place as team captain. No more of this "winning-isn't-everything" stuff. We needed to kick some butt. We needed to return to our rightful place at the top of the corporate pack. We vowed to win the following year.

I looked for men who could run 5-6 minute miles and women who could run 5½ -7 minutes. Finding the men was relatively easy; at Nike there were many former collegiate middle- and long-distance runners, including All-Americans, an American record holder, even a few Olympians.

Finding five high-caliber women runners in the 1980s, however, was more difficult. At the time, Nike female employees with collegiate distance-running experience hardly existed because even though Title IX, the equal-opportunity law, had been on the books for more than a decade, experienced women runners weren't in the Nike workforce yet. The 1984 Olympics were the first Games that women were allowed to run longer than 1500 meters.

The women on our team were an eclectic bunch that included a dancer, "lunchtime runners," and athletes from other sports. However, they were fast, much faster than the women on the teams that we competed against.

A winning team requires more than just runners; it requires great drivers, which over the years, included, legendary Nelson Farris, Woody, my wife Mary, and Paul Geis, my sophomore-year roommate. When people recognized Geis behind the steering wheel I'd say, "Yeah, our team is so good that we have an Olympian … as our driver."

They thought driving for 17 hours would be boring, but quickly discovered they were constantly moving. Each roughly five-mile leg at six-minutes-per-mile pace meant there was about half an hour between handoffs. That left very little time to park, pick up the incoming runner, find any stragglers, and drive the five miles to the next exchange point—and, of course, keep repeating that process.

The race outgrew Pacific City as the finish line. In 1989, the finish was moved north to Seaside. Team members increased from 11 to 12, the distance from 165 to 200 miles, and the limit for total number of teams from 500 to 750. To say it was wild would be an understatement. It was controlled chaos; OK, plain chaos that was occasionally controlled.

I brainstormed with teammates such as Farris, Taylor, and Roth about how to field more than just the single Tarahumara team; we wanted more participation. The result? We grew the number of Nike Corporate teams from one to six.

The key was recruiting new team captains. Throughout the summer we met at a local tavern on Thursday afternoons over a few pitchers of beer to plan and prepare. We rented vans and rooms at the beach, purchased tee-shirts and hats, and spread the cost across the various departments where we worked; if anyone questioned the expenses after they were recorded, we would ask for forgiveness.

I prepared the new team captains. "Look, something beyond your control will go wrong, which will feel awful, say, at 3:30 in the morning. You'll learn a lot about yourself and each other in how you respond."

"Got an example?" asked Marla Murray, team captain for Nike One Time Only.

"Sure. One year the traffic going into the exchange points was so congested that the backup was at least a half mile long at each exchange. We knew we'd never get the van there in time. I, along with three other runners, jumped out and jogged and hitch-hiked to our respective handoffs; we didn't miss a one. The van picked us up later."

The planning came together nicely; six teams, 66 Nike runners, 12 vans with drivers. Tarahumara won its division for the fifth time in six years. Marla found me on the beach.

"How'd it go?" I asked.

"We had to drop out. Everything was going well until we pulled the van over on a very soft shoulder. It tipped over."

My eyes widened. "Is everyone OK?"

"Just shaken up, more embarrassed than hurt. I was hoping that we'd go unnoticed. But, of course, we had a big swoosh on the van so everyone knew it was Nike. We were waving others to drive on—you know, 'nothing to see here.' Help was on the way, and then a Portland TV news helicopter circled overhead broadcasting our embarrassment to the Northwest."

She shook her head. "I know that you said something

would go wrong, and it certainly did. We wanted to finish and decided it didn't have to be this year. So, sign us up for next year, we're all in; call us One Time Only, Again."

I was feeling pretty good about our six teams, until just before Christmas in 1989 when I was summoned to the office of Del Hayes, the man who hired me in 1977, now on the board of directors. I had no idea what he wanted and approached him with extreme nervousness.

"What do you know about Hood to Coast?" he asked.

Uh-oh, where was this going?

I explained the HTC basics that he surely already understood; that we had 66 employees sharing a common running experience; that we were connecting to our Nike roots; and that it gave us the chance to mix with the local running community.

"Why do you ask?"

"The Accounting Department saw some curious expenses from various areas that referenced Hood to Coast, and I asked them to pull all the documents."

He spread out the purchase orders and invoices including tee shirts, hats, entry fees, and hotel bills. "Can you explain these?"

Uh-oh again. Not uh-oh as in I'd better get a cardboard box for my office supplies, but that I definitely had some explaining to do. Like Frank Abagnale Jr. (Leonard DiCaprio) in *Catch Me If You Can*, in the back of my mind, I'd always worried that the FBI (Tom Hanks) would someday come for me. Now, here it was, in the form of the imposing-looking Hayes.

"We had team captain meetings before this year's race and we thought it would be good to represent Nike in distinctive Nike gear," I said. "Plus, we thought it was a good use of discretionary travel and entertainment dollars."

There was a deafening silence, lasting way too long. Finally, Del burst out in his infectious laugh. I exhaled.

"It's fine," he said. "Perfect, in fact. But you don't need to go underground. Put together a plan with a budget for next year, I'll pay."

I did so. We added two more teams, including a team from Weiden & Kennedy, our ad agency. We were officially above board, endorsed by senior leadership—a formerly underground operation, now, like the race itself, running over-ground—most of it, of course, paved.

"One more condition," he said. "I'd like you to include my daughter, Kathy, on your Hood to Coast team."

That would be a problem. Not because of her ability; Kathy held the UO records at 5000 and 10000 meters and was the 1984 NCAA 10000 meter champion. Instead, it was because she wasn't a Nike employee and, therefore, couldn't run on a corporate team. Two years later we cleared that hurdle with an Open Mixed team called Nike Team Swoosh, composed of an impressive list of mostly former UO men and women distance runners, including former 5000-meter world record holder, Kathy Mills-Parker (Penn State), wife of future CEO Mark Parker. Team Swoosh was so strong that it easily won its division and set a course record, 5:44 pace, which may never be broken in the mixed division.

In 1993, our famous fellow Nike employee, Alberto Salazar, an-ex Duck who had won both the New York and Boston marathons, accepted our invitation to run on Tarahumara. It was—fitting, as you'll see—that the same year Nelson Mandela won the Nobel Peace Prize for his work in South Africa.

Our group of guys had a regular Saturday 10-mile run and Alberto, who'd recently moved from Eugene to Portland, joined us one week, already knowing many of us from his running days as a Duck. There was always much talk of cross-country, track, Hood to Coast, and other random memories.

Dave Taylor pulled Alberto into the conversation regarding the runner's suggestion that he might be finished racing.

"Al, your racing career isn't over yet. You just need to race longer distances, ultra-marathons, 50 to 100 miles."

Alberto seemed to ignore the advice, remaining silent until the subject changed, but weeks later he had news for us.

"I entered the Comrades Ultra-Marathon."

"What's that?" someone asked.

"A 56-mile race in South Africa. A friend recommended it and I decided to give it try."

After wrapping up our run, we walked to our cars.

"Alberto," I asked. "Where's your car?"

"Home. I ran from there."

"How far is that?

"Ten miles."

"You ran 10 miles here, 10 with us, and you're doing another 10 home—30 total?"

"No, 40. I'll run 10 miles more on the treadmill when I get home."

We didn't see Alberto for months, then, in May 1994, we learned that he had won Comrades. Maybe he did have a second racing career after all. Soon after returning, Salazar joined us on a run. We gave him a round of congratulatory applause.

"How'd it go?" someone asked

"Hardest race I've ever run," Alberto said. This from a man who nearly died after winning the Boston Marathon. "I'm proud of my Boston and New York marathons but if I had to pick one as my proudest accomplishment, it would be Comrades."

I quizzed him about his experience.

"The press wrote horrible things about me," he said. "They said I was washed up, I didn't know what I was getting myself into, it was just a publicity stunt for Nike South Africa. They said I would only run a handful of miles and drop out. I told them I was there to win."

"What was the race like?"

"Comrades switches direction each year and this year it started in Durban, which was the uphill direction. Imagine running from Portland towards Beaverton, through the tunnel and up Highway 26, the long, steep grade, to the top of Sylvan. That's hard! Now, multiply that four times."

"Sounds like a killer."

"Yeah, we started in the dark. I didn't know anyone. Runners started like it was the beginning of a 10k—fast. In the darkness I couldn't see anyone for a while. Runners started coming into view. I started passing them and I was in the lead at about the half-marathon and running comfortably in the lead at the marathon distance."

"How fast were you?" I asked. I had run four marathons, two in just under three hours.

"Probably about 2½-hour marathon pace. That's 5:45 pace through 52 miles. At one point I thought about dropping out and walked a few steps. But I had to finish, had to prove this wasn't a publicity stunt and that I wasn't washed up. I prayed out loud, and found the strength to win."

"Is this the start of your ultra-marathon career?"

"No," Alberto hastened to say, "it's the end of my ultra-marathon career!"

"Congratulations then," I said, "you're retiring undefeated."

Alberto still wanted to compete, not in ultra-marathons but on an HTC team that could win it all.

John Truax, a Nike employee, had captained the non-corporate team called Nike Mambu Baddu, which won the overall race. Alberto wanted to be on that team. Word got out that Mambu Baddu was putting together an even faster team for 1994—with Alberto as the anchor.

Cross-town rival Adidas quietly plotted how they could bring in some of their best runners from around the world to beat Nike. Alberto caught wind of the plan and in "Just Do It" fashion, recruited the best Nike runners he could find.

In 1994, Nike Mambu Baddu and Adidas Rolling Thunder went head-to-head for just under 16 hours in the closest and fastest race in Hood to Coast history. Mambu Baddu narrowly won, averaging exactly 5 minutes per mile.

A week later, Phil Knight flew the Mambu Baddu team back to Beaverton to honor them on the Nike campus, and to present Alberto with a black convertible BMW. Phil wanted to showcase the importance of their effort, beating Adidas in Nike's backyard.

He walked down the line of world-class runners, asking about their experiences, which turned out to be either love or hate.

"I loved it! Running is usually an individual sport and I ran on a team."

"I hated it! I'll never do it again, and I wouldn't recommend it to anyone."

"I'd run it again. We covered 200 miles of beautiful Oregon scenery."

"This was the hardest thing I ever did, worse than a marathon. I ran three hard 10ks with very little rest in a packed, sweaty van."

Adidas surrendered—at least in my mind—and didn't field a team the following year. Mambu Baddu won again, going even faster, 4:51 pace, and retired the team with a course record 15:44:55, which will be tough to beat.

Over the years it was clear that Nike people from around the world loved their Hood to Coast experiences. When in Glasgow, Scotland I visited the Nike store. On the back wall in the store were bib numbers from various road races, and among them was one from HTC. As I pointed it out to Mary, a store clerk let me know it was his number. He had applied to run on a Nike Europe HTC team and was accepted. He said his trip to Oregon, to the Nike campus, to Eugene, and the race was one of his best lifetime memories.

My knees couldn't keep up with my desire to run, so in 2002, at forty-nine, I switched to walking Portland to Coast; 130 miles instead of 200, two legs each instead of three, finishing with the runners on the beach at Seaside. I was still a runner in heart and mind.

Our Master's walking team had some of the most tenured people at Nike, both active and retired. Bob Harold, former Nike CFO and one of our fastest walkers, found that even walking teams will have something go wrong. In the middle of the night, Bob pulled our van to the side of the road to support one of our walkers but wound up in a ditch.

It jolted me awake. My wife Mary, napping in the far back seat, slid onto a teammate to her right. She didn't immediately know who was driving; I'm glad it wasn't me. She felt the jolt and heard a stream of profanity come from Bob; the van was stuck.

After calling a tow truck, Bob and I leaned against the van, looking up at the stars in the 4 a.m. darkness, silently waiting as we listened to the quick pitter-patter of steps as walkers glided by. I wanted say something of comfort to Bob, then realized what that might be. Our team name was T-Wrecks and we had a tall plywood dinosaur mounted on the top of each van. Forgetting about the dino one year, I had entered a low clearance drive-through.

"Hey," I said. "No worries. Remember, I was the guy who decapitated the Dino."

He laughed.

"Steve, do you think people will forget this?"

"Never."

Just hours before his final race, Pre, weirdly, announced to the three of us that it was time for him to give up the Great Race plaque, which he'd kept for nearly six months. Weirder still, he insisted we pose for a group shot, getting a neighbor to take the photo. Eight hours later, he was dead. Left to right, Matt Centrowitz, me, Pre, and Mark Feig.

PART IV
REFLECTIONS

We do not remember days, we remember moments.

Cesare Pavese

Chapter 15
'Without Limits'

It was a quiet evening in fall 1995, the year of two movie favorites, *Apollo 13 and Toy Story,* and I was at my desk catching up on e-mails when the phone rang.

"Steve Bence," the caller said slowly and deliberately, "this is Kenny Moore."

"Oh my gosh," I said, gushing like a star-struck twelve-year-old, "you're one of my heroes!"

But why was he calling me?

"I'm writing a movie script about Pre, *Without Limits,* and could use your help. You were about his age and knew him better than I did."

Kenny, ten years older than me, had a brilliant 25-year career writing about athletics for *Sports Illustrated.* He had placed fourteenth in the 1968 Mexico City Olympics marathon, fourth in the 1972 Munich Olympic marathon, and had held an American record in the marathon. Both Moore and Pre were University of Oregon runners, Pre from Marshfield High and Kenny from North Eugene, only about a hundred miles apart.

"Of course, however I can help."

"There's a Disney version in progress, *Prefontaine,* written by Steve James, who did Hoop Dreams. Nancy Alleman is the girlfriend in his version. I'd like Mary Marckx to be in mine." "Mine" was being produced by no less than Tom Cruise.

Pre, it turned out, had two girlfriends—at least. Mary Marckx—her last name ended with the rare "kx" combo—was the only one that I saw with Pre—or knew about. Marckx, and my wife Mary—whom Marckx calls by her maiden name, Jacko—grew up in the same neighborhood in northeast Portland. Marckx was two years older than Jacko, went to the same St. Rita Catholic Church, and crossed paths with my Mary at Marycrest Catholic High School. They both rushed the same Kappa Alpha Theta sorority at UO, both were presidents their respective senior years, and both dated runners on the Oregon track team named Steve. We even double-dated.

"You've got to have Marckx in the movie," I agreed.

"Do you know Mary well enough to ask her permission to be included in the script? She told us she doesn't want to get involved with either movie; said had put that part of her life behind her. But perhaps if you talked with her … ."

I knew Marckx well. In 1980 she became the godmother of our first child, Lynn, when we lived in Maine.

She had left Oregon abruptly after Pre's death in 1975, but had come back and been Phil Knight's secretary for a while. Then she had moved to the East Coast, still working for Nike, then Europe, before moving back to Oregon. She had dated for a while, then stopped. I wasn't sure that she had put that part of her life behind her—and, frankly, I'm not sure I had.

"I'll ask her, tell her that Pre's story needs her voice."

The 1995 award-winning documentary *Fire on the Track,*

produced by Geoff Hollister, was about Pre, which sparked interest in Hollywood to make a full-length movie; both Disney and Warner Brothers were pursuing it. Usually, in such cases, one company backs off; that wasn't the case here. Both fully intended on producing films, even if their competitor's version might come out at the same time. It was like Pre and Geis coming down homestretch in that low-key two-mile in Corvallis, the major difference being that if they finished neck-and-neck, they certainly weren't going to be holding hands.

I was eager to contribute to either movie or both. But, first, I needed to go see Phil; I needed clarity about where he stood on the two movies. When I arrived for my meeting with him, he was on the couch just outside his office. I was two minutes late.

"You used up two minutes of your time, Bence," he said, tapping on his watch.

He wasn't angry, just not one to waste time. He stood up and ushered me into a nearby conference room.

"What are we talking about?" Phil asked.

"The two Prefontaine movies."

"I'm aware."

He leaned forward, clearly interested in where this might be going

"Hollister is working with Disney and asked me to send any clothing that I might have from the early '70s," I said. "I went through my closet and loaned what I thought was relevant: tees, uniforms, a UO rain jacket, and sweats. They made copies and returned everything.

"Then out of left field, Kenny Moore called to ask for my help on his movie. I sent him the same '70s clothing that I loaned to Disney and offered anything more that I could do to be helpful. He wanted me to ask Mary Marckx to allow her character to be in the movie. She'd already declined."

"Ha!" said Phil, knowing, from the days when she worked for him, that Marckx could be stubborn and strong-willed.

"Good luck convincing Marckx to do anything she doesn't want to. Did you ask her?"

"I called," I said. "We've been friends since our college days. She challenged me, asked the tough questions, but eventually agreed because she knows how important this is to me."

His eyebrows raised. "I'm impressed," he said. "She wasn't that agreeable with me. OK, so, how do I fit into all of this?"

"I'd like to know Nike's official position on the two movies."

Phil didn't think long.

"Nike won't choose one movie over the other and we'll stay above the fight. We don't know which of the movies will be good, if either. I'd love to see at least one good movie about Pre; two would be even better. You, Hollister, and any other Nike employee can get involved as you'd like, but it will be on your own time."

I was good with that. "Can you let others know what you just said?" I asked. "The sparring between the two camps is already getting ugly."

"I'll send a memo to those who need to know, including Geoff."

"Perfect."

I was relieved to have his clarity—even if I'd been two minutes late.

The Disney team had the support of the Prefontaine family. The film would be shot at the University of Puget Sound in Tacoma, Washington. The Warner Brothers version would be filmed on location at Hayward Field. Mary stayed at Kenny's house in Hawaii, collaborating on the movie while she worked on a book of her own about Pre, which has never been published.

Kenny spoke highly of director Robert Towne, an accomplished writer, an Academy Award winner for his original screenplay for *Chinatown*, and a well-known script doctor.

"How did you and Robert get to know each other so well?" I asked Kenny.

"We worked together on *Personal Best* in the early '80s, also filmed at Hayward Field. I contributed on the athletic parts of the movie. Robert needed Bowerman's support, which I arranged, although Bill wasn't as supportive after he saw the movie, which included nudity and a lesbian relationship."

"I've never seen it; I should rent it."

"I'll warn you," Kenny said, "I'm in the movie, including full-frontal nudity."

I laughed. "Now I'll definitely have to rent it."

"A friend of mine watched it," he said, "and was surprised to see how much screen time I had. He said, 'I didn't expect you to have such a big role, yet such a small part.'"

I laughed again, even harder.

I thought Robert was fully engaged in the writing process, but apparently not. I was surprised when Kenny shared Towne's feedback about the script Moore had written.

"Robert said my 300-page script was too long," said Kenny. "He has a rule-of-thumb that each page equals about one minute of screen time, which means I just wrote a five-hour movie. It has to be less than two hours."

I came to realize that the screenwriting process was like a relay race, and it was now Robert's turn to take the baton to compress Kenny's 300 pages into a tight 120-minute movie by cutting some 60 percent of what Kenny had written.

Robert asked me about my typical day-in-the-life as an Oregon runner in the early '70s. I had saved my detailed training diaries from twenty-five years earlier so typed up what I thought was interesting, especially anything I had written specifically about Prefontaine or Bowerman. Robert circled what he thought was good and worked my memories into various scenes.

Among them was a training-run scene during which Pre created the route as we ran, at times jerking us left and right without notice, causing us to bump into each other. Another was Bowerman grabbing me by the neck to take my pulse during a track interval workout and insisting I wait for my heart rate to settle before doing my next 330. There was the 1974 fight with the AAU in Oulu, Finland, when Feig was not allowed to race, but it was changed to be about Pre. I was asked for my high school ribbons and medals for a scene in Pre's high school bedroom. Of course, I still had all that stuff; I'm a collector.

Kenny and Robert worked Marckx's recollections into the script, among the fine details that Pre's mother, Elfriede, kept plastic covers on the furniture even when guests like Dellinger arrived. Elfriede had been born in Germany before World War II, and married Ray in 1948, moving from Germany to Coos Bay. Pre understood German, which was worked into the script in Munich.

Robert often said that the story belonged to Pre's people, and he wanted to get it right.

In the summer of 1996, Marckx and I were invited to be on set during the filming of *Without Limits* in Eugene. I timed my five-week Nike sabbatical to be at the same time. I abided by Phil's edict that I do this on my own time, and I justified my first Nike sabbatical as a great way to experience and learn from a different industry, the movie industry, about a sports topic that I knew about and cared deeply about, Pre.

Marckx didn't want to stay overnight, so we teamed up for daily trips to Eugene. We met just south of Portland, off I-5, and I drove the two hours down and back, four hours for us to talk about anything and everything—not that talking was my strength. Marckx, fortunately, turned me into less of an introvert. My friends in college called me Bencie. Marckx called me Bee and my wife either Jay or Jacko.

"Remind me, Bee, when did you and Jacko first meet?" she said on one drive.

"My junior year. Mary was a sophomore in the Theta house. Scott Dahlberg was on the track team, dating one of your

Theta sisters, Mindy, and they wanted to set us up a blind date."

"When was that?"

"During the 1974 track season. I suggested that we meet after a track meet on a Saturday night, but Mary already had a date, so we met on a Sunday evening instead. Feig and I cooked the best dinner the we knew how: pork chops with sides. We sat on the carpeted floor because we didn't have enough dining room chairs. Mary knocked over her wine glass, and was so embarrassed. As we cleaned it up, I took the blame that we had to sit on the floor in the first place. After everyone left, Mark let me know that I needed to hold on to her, that she was someone special. From that day onward, Feig always introduced Mary as 'Steve's girlfriend' and I eventually became comfortable with that. And here we are, married."

Mary laughed at the story, making me relax.

On one of our drives, as we talked of Pre, Marckx turned particularly serious.

"Bee, my hardest day was when I went to Coos Bay for Steve's funeral. I wanted to be with his family and, instead, found them consoling Nancy. I had no idea he had another girlfriend. I was crushed. I drove back to Eugene, skipped the memorial at Hayward Field, packed my car, and drove south the next morning. Later I read about his other girlfriends. When did he have time for all of this?"

"News to me," I said. "I thought it was just you."

"I still feel Steve's spiritual presence. I believe the two of us are connected beyond this life, both the past and future. Everyone probably thinks I'm nuts. Robert listened to me talk about my spiritual beliefs—probably didn't understand nor believe what he heard—but he worked that into the script anyway."

I found four times in the script where Robert addressed Mary's beliefs, the first in the café scene where they discuss a possible past-life connection between them.

PRE
There's just something about you that I recognize.

MARY
Like haven't we met somewhere before?

PRE
No, that we haven't met before, but I feel we have.
Like you're a stranger, but you're familiar.

The second time was the cemetery scene, regarding the strength of Mary's belief.

PRE
Are you Catholic?

MARY
Lots of people are.

PRE
Lots of people say they are, but I bet you really are.

MARY
I'm not sure I understand what you mean. Should I be flattered or insulted?

PRE
No, I wasn't insulting you! It's the hardest thing in the world to believe in something. If you do, it's a miracle. There's always somebody trying to talk you out of what you believe. Anybody. Everybody. Your own mother.

I didn't know Pre's mother, Elfriede, but the movie portrays her as being hesitant to support his decision to run in college.

The third time in the script was when Pre talked to Bowerman.

PRE
I'd like to ask you something.

BOWERMAN
OK.

PRE
How do you and Barbara ... I mean do you pretty
much believe in the same things?

Bowerman looks up, shocked.

BOWERMAN
Good God, Pre. I have no idea. The woman's a
complete mystery to me.

PRE
Well ... how come you ... get along so well?

BOWERMAN
I don't have to know what she believes in. I believe
in her.

Pre suddenly smiles, and starts to walk out.

BOWERMAN
You're easily pleased, I must say.

The fourth and final time was when they talked at the end
of the movie. Just before Pre died, he said to Mary, "I'm not
going to let you go.'"

It was fascinating to see the movie team come together
in Eugene. Kenny, of course, had deep knowledge of the UO
running community and insisted that the movie be authentic
to runners, which he knew how to do. And insisted that it
appeal to non-runners, too, which Robert knew how to do.
An empty space in the industrial outskirts of western
Eugene was rented and staff came from all over the the

country: Production, Accounting, Art, Camera, Construction, Costumes, Make Up, Hair, Grip, Lighting, Locations, Sound, and more. It was like a mini-city—a really small military base without the military.

Marckx and I walked through the building, talking to people as we toured. I was impressed with the attention to detail; the movie storyboard on the wall, wardrobe from the 1970s, and the editing of film, all coming together so the film would flow seamlessly between the filming being done now and historical film.

We were asked if we wanted to sit in on the "daily," a screening of what had been filmed the previous day. Absolutely! We watched as Conrad Hall, an Oscar-winning cinematographer (*Butch Cassidy and the Sundance Kid*), and others geeked out, congratulating and critiquing themselves as they studied their work. On one day we were there, the scene being filmed was a slow-motion zoom on the bloodied shoe of Pre (played by Billy Crudup) as he ran down the homestretch, with a cut foot, to win the three-mile race at the 1970 NCAA Track & Field Championships in Des Moines (13:22.0).

I turned to a knowledgeable staff person. "You know Pre actually cut his foot at a motel swimming pool, right? Why did Robert write it as a sex-related injury in a motel room?"

"I don't know, maybe he changed a boring truth into an over-the-top scene about Pre's womanizing."

Marckx was apprehensive as we entered a room to meet blonde actress Monica Potter, who would play Mary in the movie. Monica, who would go on to play Kristina Braverman in the hit TV show Parenthood from 2010 to 2015, was down-to-earth, modest, and beautiful. As we left, Mary nodded her head at me.

"She'll do!" she said, with her characteristic laugh.

Cruise, the producer, considered playing the role of Prefontaine but decided that at age thirty-four he was too old. Cruise/Wagner Productions, the company founded by Cruise and business partner Paula Wagner, agreed, along with Robert, to cast the relatively inexperienced Crudup, then twenty-eight. When told that Crudup wished to talk to us, Mary and I went to his trailer, where we found him in full Prefontaine character, including a wig.

In the two-hour session, Mary provided wonderful insights about Pre's personality. She could channel what he said, what she saw, his relationships with his coaches, teammates, and family.

When it was my turn to add nuance, I stressed how much Pre changed after his fourth-place finish at the 1972 Olympics.

"Pre went to Munich cocky that he would win, and devastated when he didn't," I told Crudup. "It took months for him to come around. Once he did, he emerged less cocky, but still very confident. And yeah, his swagger returned. After the Olympics, Pre seemed to care more about others, including me, and wasn't as self-centered as he'd been. He even cared more about his competitors, who he usually beat, turning around to talk to those behind him before taking his victory lap."

After we left, Mary shook her head sideways.

"That," she said, "was creepy. I really thought I was talking with Steve. Billy is good."

I agreed. "It's like we both aged twenty years since Pre's death, but he'll always be twenty-four to us and his fans."

The person in charge of casting athletes did an exceptional job, bringing in elite runners to add to the authenticity of the movie. US Olympian Pat Porter played Lasse Viren. In my mind, the only athlete who was questionable was Steve Ave, a solid runner who played silver medalist Mohammed Gammoudi of Tunisia. Gammoudi was small at 5'8", and Ave was more than 6', maybe around 6'2". When I watched the Olympic race, I could tell which was real footage and which was reenacted by tracking the shorter #904 Gammoudi against the taller Ave.

I loved the final version of the Olympic race, a blend of beautiful cinematography with music.

"In that 5000 meters final, there are 13 runners," said Towne, "but they are a single body. They're suffering so closely together, sharing pain, they develop a peculiar camaraderie that you don't find anywhere else."

I had lunch with a runner who'd been cast in the movie, Jeff Atkinson. He had made the 1500 meter finals of the 1988 Seoul Olympics but failed to make the 1996 USA Olympic team. He came to Eugene, when asked, to play ... me.

"Jeff," another runner said to him as we were eating. "I heard you have a speaking part."

"Yep," he said, pointing to me. "I'm Steve Bence."

All seemed to be going well—until it wasn't. One morning, while on our drive to Eugene, Mary seemed uncharacteristically upset.

"What's up?" I asked her.

"I'm going to talk to Robert. I want my name taken out of the movie."

"Why? What's bothering you?"

"Bee, if I didn't know who that character is, I wouldn't know it was me; it's all wrong. I'll speak my mind. Watch me, I won't back down."

Mary was warming up for a confrontation. After the day's filming, the three of us met at McMenamins North Bank Restaurant on the Willamette River. Robert looked exhausted from the day's work. He ordered a stiff drink to relax. Mary returned from outdoors where she'd smoked a cigarette to calm herself.

"Robert," she said, "I have something I need to say."

His weary eyes said "not now" but Mary wasn't about to back off.

"The character you've created isn't me. When the movie comes out, my friends will either think that I didn't represent myself correctly or that you didn't listen well enough. Either way, it isn't good. So, call her Susan or whatever you want, but don't call her Mary."

"Mary, I can do that. But if we can find a compromise that we both can live with, the movie will be better. Are you willing to work with me?"

She exhaled. "Sure."

"Let's have dinner. You think about the scene that offends you the most. After dinner we'll go to my hotel room and talk it through until we have a solution, even if we go to two o'clock in the morning. And promise me you won't be so fucking stubborn."

Not bothered in the least, Mary nodded her head, laughed, and the conversation shifted.

We settled into Robert's spacious room in the downtown Hilton.

"So," Robert said, "did you pick a scene?"

"Yes, the one that bothers me most is when I'm in the church kneeling, praying in front of the candles. I think I know why you did that; I've seen scenes like that in old movies, but all my friends know that I never went to church while I was in Eugene."

Robert asked questions as though he was leading a therapy session.

"How often did you go to church growing up?"

"Every Sunday with my family."

"Did you go to public school?"

"No, I went to Central Catholic High School."

"You had a religious upbringing and the two of you developed a deep relationship. I have 120 minutes to tell this story, and even though that scene—which, by the way, is less than a minute long— didn't literally happen, it shows the religious, spiritual person of who you were."

Mary seemed to accept that explanation and moved on to her next complaint.

"In general, my character comes across weak. I wouldn't

take any crap from Pre."

"OK, I'll add a scene with you're standing up to him."

Robert wrote and filmed a scene with "actress" Mary giving Pre the riot act just outside his trailer, and the "real" Mary was pleased. Later, Robert explained that he had to drop it because he had already written a tense scene between Pre and Bowerman, and another such scene would convey too much fighting. Though Mary was disappointed, I was surprised that she seemed OK, satisfied that Robert had listened to her and made the effort. I think she was actually letting go of her past.

A couple weeks into the filming Mary and I felt as if we were only getting in the way. As Kenny, then Robert, wrote and rewrote the script, they welcomed our input. But once filming started, even though they asked our opinion after calling out "cut," they didn't make any adjustments based on our feedback.

We decided it was time to stop going to Eugene; we weren't wallowing in self-pity, just facing the fact that they seemed to have everything under control. Several days passed when my phone rang. It was Towne's assistant.

"Robert wants to know where you are."

"We just sensed we weren't needed anymore."

"Robert says he'd like to have you here."

I called Mary. Our I-5 trips were back on.

"I think our role has changed from advisors to cheerleaders," I told her.

Robert developed a relationship with Bowerman and started to understand him better. Donald Sutherland played Bill in the movie.

"I just spent hours with Bill and rewrote parts of the script," said Robert. "The story will be strengthened, especially the relationship he had with Pre. I coached Sutherland about Bill's true character, which isn't a typical coach. It didn't take long, Sutherland gets him now."

After the movie was completed, Warner Brothers encouraged me to arrange local screenings in support of a word-of-mouth promotion. Bowerman attended one such showing with his wife Barbara and their three sons Tom, then fifty-two; Jay, fifty-six; and Jon, sixty. Before the screening, in the theater lobby, Barbara came up and thanked me.

"Steve, this is a big event. Not necessarily the movie, but this is the first time in years that the boys have been together."

The Bowerman brothers sat a few rows behind me, and I listened for their reaction. Late in the movie when Bill and Pre had a heated discussion that ends with Pre telling Bill, "Did it ever occur to you that I might know something about myself that you don't? You vain, inflexible, son of a bitch! You don't know me any better than you know yourself. And you're never going to change *you*, Bill."

The brothers laughed, which seemed odd. Back in the lobby after the screening, I chatted with the three, who said they'd liked the movie.

"Why did you laugh when Pre confronted your father?" I asked. "That part wasn't supposed to be funny."

"Because it's something we always wanted to tell our dad, but we were afraid. It was perfect."

In late August 1998, a premiere for *Without Limits* was held in Eugene, delayed a year to distance itself from the other Prefontaine movie, which released in 1997; Warner Brothers wanted to wait for its own moment in the sun. Cruise was greeted by swarms of screaming fans.

On September 8, 1998, the main premiere was set for the Mann Theater in Los Angeles; Marckx, Mary, and I packed our formal wear and flew to L.A. There was a large turnout, including many celebrities we recognized: Jenna Elfmann, Cuba Gooding Jr, and Kevin Bacon. We were invited to the party afterwards, for which we decided to arrive fashionably late and disappear into the crowd to people-watch.

As we checked in at the desk, hoping our names were actually on the list, a support staff member recognized Marckx.

"Mary Marckx!" she shouted from across the room. "There you are. Come with me. Tom Cruise has been looking for you."

Marckx, totally surprised, looked at Mary and me. We waved her to move on without us, and she was whisked into a separate room, a big smile on her face; how many times does someone say out loud to you, "Tom Cruise has been looking for you?" Mary and I watched through the doorway as she and Cruise had a long conversation. Later, she said Cruise had told her how appreciative he was of everything she'd done to make the movie a success.

Back at the hotel, we unwound. It was a great day and we reflected on the roller-coaster ride of emotions over the previous two years. And now it was over.

Following the film, Mary Marckx felt compelled to do something she hadn't done for years: start dating again. She wanted us to get to know her new boyfriend, Jim Creel. From time to time, we met for drinks or a meal. Jim had two daughters from a previous marriage and his hobby was music; one of our get-togethers involved listening to him play at a local tavern. The two got engaged; Mary was about to become an instant mother of two teenagers. We celebrated with them on their wedding night.

During the toasts, Marckx found me in the crowd and raised her glass.

"Bee, raise your hand." People turned to look. "The two of us spent many hours together during the making of the Without Limits movie. We must have driven together from Portland to Eugene and back fifty times. One of the biggest things I learned was how much I missed male companionship. I did something about it, and here I now am with Jim. Thank you, Bee."

If I hadn't been sure Marckx had put the past behind her, I was now.

I lifted my glass.

"To Mr. and Mrs. Creel. Cheers!"

Chapter 16
The Unfinish Line

Covid hit. I started working from home in March 2020, and it was now April 2021, near the end of a year-plus "hunkering down" that had left Mary and me as restless as collegians hankering for a spring-break trip.

"Let's drive to Eugene," I said. "Do you realize we've slept in the same bed for over a year?"

"That's crazy," Mary acknowledged. "Sounds perfect."

There was something comforting about the two-hour drive south on Interstate-5. Timely. Right. Familiar. The past year had felt like the longest, yet shortest, year of our lives. Now, we were headed back to where our journey had begun nearly half a century before.

A BBC reporter had once asked me, "If Pre could go to Eugene thirty years after his death, what would he think?"

"He would feel at home," I told him. "Not much has

changed."

Once in Eugene, we approached the campus. I turned south onto Agate Street from Franklin Boulevard—and gasped. Everything had changed!

"What?" said Mary, looking panicked.

"Sorry. I wasn't ready for what I'm now seeing. This is spectacular."

Ahead of us lay the new Hayward Field, the moment reminding me of Dorothy in *The Wizard of Oz* seeing the Emerald City for the first time. It was beautiful, futuristic, majestic, inviting. If only I was a runner in college again.

"Why are you so surprised?" Mary asked. "You've been following the new construction."

"It's just that now it became real for me. I'm happy with it."

I flashed back fifty years to the Friday evening of my freshman year when I had walked across the street from my dorm room to sit alone for hours in the Hayward Field stands, reflecting on how lucky I was, and vowing to do my best.

Over the past century, others had their own Hayward Field stories: athletes, coaches, fans, media, volunteers. Some didn't think the hallowed stands should have been replaced. But I understood: the old, rotting, wooden structure had to be torn down. It was time. It was now all gone: the East Grandstands, West Grandstands, Bowerman Building—everything had been replaced by a shiny new stadium that looked both elegant and exotic, as if it was a silver-wood spacecraft that could suddenly take off after briefly touching down on earth.

The younger athletes I'd talked to loved the new stadium. Friends my age had mixed feelings about replacing the iconic structure; to some, it was like replacing Fenway Park with a soul-less, futuristic structure that said nothing. But, I reminded them: that's what time does. Imbues a place with a history all its own. Hell, Hayward itself had once been new and soul-less.

"This is a huge step forward," I said to Mary. "There are those who will struggle with this change. Now it's up to the next generations to build on the past and create something better for the next hundred years."

I was excited about the change; after all, change had been a constant in my life. It had been my father's choice to follow a military career, relocating every couple of years. We were always leaving people and places behind; that's why leaving the old Hayward didn't bother me. In my eyes, that's just how life worked.

But amid my personal changes in my post-high-school years, some thing hadn't changed, like the importance of family. Even if my family members hadn't been with me—particularly my father— they were still part of my journey forward. I always wanted my father to be proud of me in school, sports, and work. He had come to all my school events, perhaps forced by my mother, and I would often hear his distinctive cough in the audience, comforting me that he was there.

He smoked, which probably contributed to his early death, and he didn't want me to smoke. Once, he had me take a long drag from one of his cigarettes; it tasted horrible, and it left me coughing uncontrollably. That, I think, was the idea: to get me to hate it.

"I don't want you to smoke," he said. "I tried to stop smoking to set a positive example for my sons, but I can't; I enjoy it too much. I don't want you to be like me. I want you to be better than me."

For some reason, such thoughts tumbled in my mind as Mary and I walked across the campus, then back to our car.

"How in the world did I end up where I am now?" I wondered aloud. "I didn't plan anything; it just happened. I wouldn't call it dumb luck or random chance. There must be a reason."

"Synchronicity?"

I often used that word to describe events that happened for a reason, their connections perhaps even spiritually imbued. Mary calls them coincidences.

"I know you're tired of me using that word," I said. "I'm happy with how everything turned out. Yet, I have so many "what-ifs?" What if I'd never come to Oregon? What if I couldn't have handled the competition? What if I'd never met you?"

"You're in one of your moods," she said, obviously wanting to avoid the conversation. "I'll drive. You think."

I took her up on the offer, my memories freshly fueled by being in Eugene, where my story had really begun; by seeing the new Hayward Field; and by visiting Pre's Rock, at which I had told his story over several decades to thousands of Nike employees.

What I realized is that my time at Oregon and at Nike—in many ways, my life—had been shaped by five people: my father, who, as I mentioned, taught me, flexibility, adaptability, and dealing with change; Bowerman; Pre; Phil; and a "player to be named later." Each had given me gifts of sorts.

Now, as we drove away from the new stadium and the tower that rose in the air in Bowerman's honor, I thought of the man. What would Bill have thought of the new Hayward Field?

He retired my sophomore year so he could focus on fundraising. The West Grandstands were decaying and had to be replaced. The grandstands were torn down after my sophomore year and the new grandstands were ready before my senior season. Originally, the new West Grandstands were planned to stretch from the finish line to the 100-meter starting line, but they fell short. One day, a knowledgeable friend had pointed to the northern end of the stands that abruptly stopped at a small parking lot.

"That's where Bowerman's money ran out," he said.

A decade after Nike stock went public, Bowerman donated $2 million for construction of the Bowerman Building on the northwest corner of Hayward Field, picking that location to block the north wind from the homestretch. There had been record-breaking performances that had to be nullified because the tailwind was over the allowable 2-meters-per-second limit.

There was just one problem with Bill's idea: the wind had to go somewhere when it hit the Bowerman Building: over it, or around it, but somewhere. Allegedly it converged where the wind measuring device was—about halfway down the final straight. It was one of the few creative ideas of Bill's that didn't work.

Frankly, I think Bowerman would have loved the new Hayward Field. He always cared about the athlete, the fans, and the community. In many ways, he was both a visionary and pioneer. In the early 1960s he introduced jogging into the United States, inviting Eugene residents to run on the Hayward Field track, with his student-athletes serving as coaches.

Bill was limited by the amount of money he could raise; I can only assume he would have been delighted at what over $200 million, perhaps as much as $270 million—the cost of the new Hayward—could have built. In Bowerman's utopia, the athletes would have priority, and the facility would be shared with the university students and the community.

So, what had Bowerman's gift to me been? From time to time, I'd been asked what part he played in helping me becoming a better runner.

"Nothing, really," I usually replied.

I wasn't being disingenuous, just honest. I avoided the man because of his legendary pranks and his failed shoe experiments. Instead, Bowerman's gift to me was a lesson on vision: how moving forward in life might have an array of moving parts but the key to making it all work was never forgetting the overall goal—while, say, you were mixing the rubber asphalt in a cement mixer to test it as a new track surface.

Bowerman's inspiration to me was the track environment that he had built over 24 years as head coach. He assembled the best assistant coaches, athletes, facilities, and shoes possible. He nurtured a knowledgeable fan base, an honorable heritage, and prided himself as a teacher of "competitive response"—

life doesn't always go as planned, things will go wrong, and quick adjustments are needed in the moment. He created an environment where everyone on the track team could rise to their potential, and many would become examples of "how to do it right"—and not just the stars like Pre.

Bob Rust, a pre-med dentistry student, ran a personal best 4:03.1 mile at the 1974 Twilight Meet, a time that would have been a school record at dozens of universities across the nation. He finished seventh that night, those in front of him all teammates.

"I'd rather be a small fish in a big pond, than a big fish in a small pond," he once said.

The team was pumped for Bob because of his excitement over his 4:03 mile. He graduated early to start his dental career—without ever running an official varsity race. And yet he still felt as if he was part of something—something unlike anywhere else in the country. Much of that, I think, was the joy of being in the environment that Bowerman created, a joy I, too, experienced. At the time, I probably took much of it for granted; over time, I realized I had the privilege of being in the right place at the right time: Bowerman's place and Bowerman's time.

Pre? He offered me the gift of unbridled passion and the honor of fighting for justice.

Phil admired the hell out of Pre, saying if Nike could have the personality of a human, he'd want it to be that of Pre. It wasn't because of what Pre did; at one point, he held every American record from 2000 meters to 10000 meters. It was because of how he did it.

UO Coach Bill Dellinger insisted Pre never missed a workout, nor a race. I witnessed his consistency when he stayed with us. I had to drag myself out of bed for my morning run, occasionally skipping a day if I could find an excuse. Pre's morning run was just a part of who he was, as much a fixture as his arms or legs. "To give anything less than your best," he said, "is to sacrifice the gift."

In 2011, I had written an article for *The Oregonian* headlined, "College football needs a Prefontaine." I compared the injustice of college football amateurism to Pre's 1970s fight against the AAU.

Football needed its own Pre, I argued, to stand up for the football players' rights to get proper compensation for their most lucrative years. My article started like this:

> In spring 1974, after Steve Prefontaine graduated from Oregon, he invited many of his teammates on the track team to join him in Europe for the summer. He assured us that we could show up, enter meets just as he had done the year before, and get paid.
>
> I was intrigued by the idea of extending my junior 800-meter season, having a summer adventure. So, I, along with seven or eight others, took Pre up on the offer. I spent nearly two months hopping through Finland and Sweden, negotiating payment with meet directors, running 16 races, and pocketing the money.
>
> After expenses, I made $133. Then I ran for Oregon my senior year.
>
> I broke the rules, both of the NCAA and the Amateur Athletic Union, which I'm acknowledging publicly for the first time. But I had reasons to do it that I think are even more relevant today.

Rachel Bachman, an *Oregonian* sportswriter at the time, coached me to write the article and suggested the sentence about breaking the rules of the NCAA and AAU. I struggled with my feelings about that sentence, admitting guilt, eventually deciding if I looked up to Pre for being outspoken, I had to speak up as well.

Being a teammate and friend of Pre changed my life. I had to deal with his death and, two years later, with my father's death. Both Pre and my father were raised in blue-collar environments and I think their work ethic, integrity, and love of family rubbed off on me.

Both of their deaths came too soon, my father's at forty-six and Pre's at twenty-four. Only a few hours before Pre had died, he'd looked at my jaw-wired face, touched my shoulder, and said, in essence, "Give it your best." In his honor, I'd tried to do exactly that in my life.

When my life transitioned from the University of Oregon to Nike, I began learning lessons from an array of people in an array of places all over the world. But nobody taught me more than Phil Knight. His gift to me was the opportunity to rise to my ability in a business environment, in a similar way that Bowerman had created an environment beneficial to me in track and field.

Nike, in essence, was the ultimate "big pond." And like Bob Rust's perspective on Oregon, I felt blessed to be swimming in it, even if I was a minnow.

Most importantly, Phil taught me how to overcome problems—how to look the monster in the eye and not blink. Anyone who has read his book, *Shoe Dog*, knows that Nike, early on, was in perpetual danger of failing. But, of course, it didn't. Phil said he loved the challenge; the bigger the problem, the bigger the opportunity.

In 1972, when BRS lost the rights to sell Tiger shoes in the US, the BRS employees, at the time, thought it was over. Phil looked at it differently. "This is great news!" he said. "We can control our own destiny—the Nike brand."

In the mid-'90s, when Nike was being attacked for the working conditions in our Asian contract factories, Phil took it personally, especially when the UO students directed their protests directly at him. In front of the National Press Club in Washington, D.C., Phil took ownership for the problems. After a few years, Nike was seen as the victor, not the villain.

In 1998, after a particularly difficult company-wide layoff,

I sat with hundreds of employees in the Tiger Woods building, waiting for Phil to take the Stanford Auditorium stage. Morale was at an all-time low. What would Phil say? Who was to blame? Phil walked up to the microphone, and paused, looking into the silent audience.

"I'm sorry," he finally said. "I took my eye off the ball. I don't know how we got here, and it won't happen again. But I can't fix this without you."

He had us!

In 2001, amid the implementation of a Nike enterprise software-solution-gone-wrong that cost Nike more than $100 million in lost sales, the stock price plummeted by 20 percent, triggering a flurry of class-action lawsuits.

Phil just shrugged. "This is what we get for $400 million, a speed bump?"

I learned, Phil didn't hide from problems; he owned them.

I've heard Phil say, "I'm never as good nor as bad as people make me out to be."

Over the years I saw Nike, in terms of the plight of factory workers, change from being the poster child of doing things wrong to the poster child of getting it right.

In 2009, Nike suffered through its largest layoff in the company's history; 5 percent of the workforce was cut—1,750 employees, including 500 in Beaverton. Four people from our Portland-to-Coast walking teams lost their jobs, making our usually festive post-race get-together at McMenamins Pub a sad one.

I arrived a few minutes late, sat down and poured myself a beer from one of the pitchers. I was surprised to see Phil, sitting next to Mike Quinn, one of our teammates who was let go.

I'd first met Quinny at our Nike factory in Maine thirty years earlier. He had moved from New England to Asia to Beaverton.

"What's Phil doing here?" I whispered to Lisa McKillips, Phil's executive admin for decades, and our team captain.

"He knows about our four people laid off," she said. "He wanted to join us."

Over the next half hour, I watched Phil move seats and privately talk one-to-one with each of the four. He then stood up to say his few final words to the rest of us.

"In good times I get all the credit; in bad times I get all the blame. Nike is more than just one person. I know that you all have your fingerprints all over this company."

Phil raised his glass. "Thank you."

He finished his beer, put down his glass, and left.

How classy, how gracious was that?

There were a few misty eyes.

Quinny couldn't help himself. "Hey, Phil left without paying the bill!"

On July 25, 2017, I celebrated my 40-year Nike anniversary as part of an event held on the Beaverton campus. Mary attended with our four adult children and several hundred others.

I was on the Tiger Woods stage with my close friends Steve Roth, Rick Lower, Dave Pearson, and Lalit Monteiro, who told stories of my career to date. There was fun, humor, jabs, irreverence, and a sincerity about my journey.

Cory, my youngest daughter, a University of Nevada, Las Vegas grad who had worked ten years at the Wynn Hotel, decided at the event that Nike was the right company for her. She applied for a job and within months would move from Las Vegas back to Beaverton and join me at Nike.

Even though I was the lone Bence on stage, other Bences in the audience lived most of those forty years with me, experiencing the highs and lows that go along with moving around the world.

Nike is a sports company, and Mary knows her sports. Our

family plans revolved around the UO sports calendar; football, basketball, softball, and track.

Mary had taken over a matriarch role when her mother died on my 50th birthday, continuing the family rituals such as Thanksgiving and Christmas. Don't ever say anything bad about her children or, for that matter, the Ducks; she is fiercely protective.

Mary is Switzerland, the neutral party holding all of us together, almost an impossible role, which includes the Woodman and Taylor families who have grown up together, three couples, traveling the world, parenting nine children born in five countries. We've been on the roller coaster of life, and, like most, have had our share of problems with all the twists and turns that go with the exhilarating ride.

Although I've tried to adopt Phil's thinking that the bigger the problem, the bigger the opportunity, I suspect that Mary would prefer the merry-go-round of life, skipping Splash Mountain to patiently wait on a bench for the rest of us.

We've been on this wild ride together—and her gift to me supersedes all the others. Mary has given me the gift of companionship over essentially a lifetime. She has been, frankly, my best friend.

She understood me when I was trying to make a mark at Oregon and did the same with Nike.

Among the highs—she experienced the joy I had competing in Sweden and Finland, launching new factory lines overseas, and the family sharing the wonderful tribute at my 40-year Nike anniversary.

And among the lows, she experienced those too: my missing out on qualifying for the 1975 NCAA Championships as a senior while racing with my jaw wired shut. (All things considered, it might have been my best race.) Then seeing me grieve Pre's death and my father's death.

She was there, my source of strength, helping me through whatever rubber-legged homestretch I was coming down.

Now, after reflecting on all these years, our trip to Eugene was all but over; we were ten minutes from home. I looked at Mary as she drove and for some reason I thought of a time months before our thirtieth anniversary, when a co-worker asked what had been the most romantic thing I'd ever done for her. I didn't have an answer.

So that evening I asked her, "What's the most romantic thing I've ever done for you?"

"You?" She laughed. "I don't know. The first thing that comes to mind is when you went to get me a sandwich when I was in the Busan Hospital."

She was referring to her hospital stay in Korea the day after delivering Cory, our fourth and final child. Mary planned to stay three nights, bonding with her newborn baby as she had done with Chris in Portland, away from me and our other children. But she wasn't enjoying her hospital stay. Few people spoke English, she was an oddity in this foreign culture, and she didn't like the Korean hospital food.

"Would you go to the Seaman's Club and get me a sandwich?" she asked.

"I'm on it," I said.

The Seaman's Club, where a lot of Nike folks hung out after work hours, catered to American tastes and what she needed now was something familiar. It was early evening and several of my Nike friends were already there having a beer, or two, or more.

"Congrats, Bence!" someone said. People clapped, patted me on the back.

"Pull up a chair, Dad!" said someone else.

"Naw, I just came to get Mary a—."

"Ah, come one, we're buying you a beer. You're a family of six now!"

"But I—"

"Bartender, bring a couple of beers for the man."

They peppered me with questions about how Mary was doing, then talked the bartender into selling them an unopened bottle of gin, knowing that Mary liked her gin and tonic.

Two hours after leaving Mary's hospital room on my mission, I returned with that bottle of gin, a gift, in hand.

"Where is the sandwich?" Mary asked.

"I forgot."

Now, Mary pulled the car into the driveway, leaving behind 1972. Leaving behind Pre, Bowerman, my father, and Phil. Leaving behind Taiwan, Korea, and other places—experiences—that had molded a kid in two-sizes-too-large spikes into something more. Thanks, in part, to a company that was right.

There is no finish line.

Acknowledgments

On August 6, 2020 I found a blank notebook, scribbled the date on the first page, and wrote, "Can I write my own book?"

Ellen Devlin, a long-time friend and colleague, encouraged me to do so; without her I would have never seriously considered writing *1972*.

I knew I couldn't do it alone. So I reached out to Bob Welch, who I'd first met when he'd been a sportswriter for *The Oregon Daily Emerald*, the UO college newspaper, and later became a columnist for *The Register-Guard* in Eugene and an author of more than 25 books. Over the next year, he became my coach, editor, and mentor; when I took a wrong turn or got stuck, Bob got me back on course. I would have been lost without him.

To our best friends, John and Kathy Woodman, and Dave and Terry Taylor. We met at the UO a half century ago, collectively lived in six Asian countries, and raised our nine children together. Our families traveled the world, tailgated at Autzen Stadium, celebrated weddings and the births of grandchildren. This story wouldn't be the same without all of you. It takes a village. Let the roller coaster ride continue!

I would like to thank three leaders in the Department of Nike Archives (DNA): Rick Shannon, Rick Lower, and Scott Reames, who met with me regarding what was seen as a hole in the telling of the Nike story, the manufacturing side. Few knew Nike's DNA at the depths that these three historians did. They said that I was the only person at Nike who could tell this story and fully supported me in any specific requests I had.

The leaders in Nike's Global Sourcing and Manufacturing organization who gave me the freedom to work on the manufacturing story which, quite frankly, is the Nike story; Mike Brewer, Jaycee Pribulsky, Greg Bui, and Ernie Rose.

Jerry Karver, who worked in Asia about the same time I did, and later was my boss, taught me much of what I've reflected in this book.

Ron Lish, Nike's General Manager in Taiwan, shared the passion of factory partnerships and storytelling. He was—and still is—a wonderful "thought partner," sounding board, and a source of perspective.

Laurie Hatch, who, when I began the documentary on Nike's manufacturing history in 2019, took care of all the details so I could focus on the story itself.

Jeff Johnson, Nelson Farris, and Lisa McKillips—some of the earliest employees at Nike—read the final draft of my book. I received seven documents from Jeff over two weeks, titled "Nitpicks #1 through Nitpicks #7," a total of fourteen pages. After seeing them, Welch e-mailed me, "Jeff really did us a huge favor. Excellent feedback."

Steve Roth, Dave Pearson, and Rick Lower comprised our Old Guys Quarterly group that made it a point to meet every three months and discuss whatever is top-of-mind. They are a part of the story and the telling of it. Two others that fit into this group are Lalit Monteiro and Patrice Thramer. Lalit was on stage with the rest of us at my 40-year anniversary and I recently teamed with Patrice on a project; she cares deeply about inspiring today's Nike employees.

Longtime Nike colleagues Jerry Hauth and Mike Buisan, who, like me, journeyed to almost every country in which we've produced shoes, and shared their lessons with me.

I'm eternally grateful to Mark Feig, my college roommate and teammate, who steered me to Mary—he was my best man at the wedding—and to Nike.

Ron Nelson, the best boss that anyone could ever hope for, is one of the smartest, most action-oriented, and most people-oriented individuals that I've ever known. Cheers, Nellie!

Because I wanted to be sure the story passed the test of authenticity and accuracy within a sophisticated running community, I had it edited by Kenny Moore, Tom Jordan, Curtis Anderson, Ken Goe, and Ron Bellamy, writers whom I respect so highly.

Finally, my wife Mary, mother Joan Bence, Mary Marckx Creel, Kathy Woodman, John Truax, and my college competitor from the University of Washington, Greg Gibson, all of whom read the semifinal draft and provided valuable feedback and caught errors galore.

Mary was initially dubious about this project, which inspired me to finish the race; it was much harder than I imagined.

Thank you, all!

Contact the author at: stevebence@icloud.com

Website: www.1972book.com

Facebook: www.facebook.com/1972.SteveBence

Bence's blog: www.stevebence.blogspot.com

.

Made in the USA
Monee, IL
11 August 2022

11458600R00142